Under the
Starfruit Tree

Under the Starfruit Tree

FOLKTALES FROM VIETNAM

told by
Alice M. Terada

illustrations by Janet Larsen

introduction and notes
by Mary C. Austin

A Kolowalu Book
University of Hawaii Press
Honolulu

94 93 92 91 90 89   5 4 3 2 1

Library of Congress Cataloging-in-Publication Data

Terada, Alice M.
    Under the starfruit tree : folktales from Vietnam / told by Alice
M. Terada ; illustrations by Janet Larsen ; introduction and notes
by Mary C. Austin.
       p.   cm. — (A Kolowalu book)
    Bibliography: p.
    Summary: Presents stories from North and South Vietnam, providing
insight into the history, culture, and religious beliefs of mountain
tribes, lowland farmers, and fishing people.
    ISBN 0–8248–1252–2 (alk. paper)
    1. Tales—Vietnam. [1. Folklore—Vietnam.] I. Larsen, Janet,
ill. II. Title.
PZ8.1.T259Un 1989
[398.2]—dc20   89–5123
                                             CIP
                                             AC

For Christine and Matthew

CONTENTS

Food, Love, and Laughter

ACKNOWLEDGMENTS

The author gratefully acknowledges the many people who have encouraged and supported the efforts of bringing this collection together. Chief among them are the translators, Tuyet Li Westerman, Than Lo Sananikone, and Nguyen Dat Thinh, all former residents of Vietnam.

Special thanks go to Ian MacMillan and Steven Goldsberry for reading and critiquing the stories at various stages, with unflagging support throughout. I was fortunate to have met Professor Tran Van Khe of the University of Paris, Sorbonne, who shared not only illustrations of the *dan bau* from his book, *Les Traditions Musicales: Viet Nam*, but also tapes of the instrument in performance.

To Mary C. Austin, Professor Emeritus, University of Hawaii, I am especially grateful. She willingly interrupted her work on annotated bibliographies of multicultural children's books in order to write the Introduction and Notes.

I deeply appreciate all the suggestions offered to me; each criticism has made the tales more accessible to the Western reader.

INTRODUCTION

Legend marks the beginnings of Vietnam and its people. Said to be "children of a dragon and grand-children of a fairy," the people trace their mythical ancestry to Lac Long Quan. Lac Long introduced a social order to the people living along the coast of the South China Sea before recorded time; he taught them to plant and plow, to cook and build. He destroyed the demons that inhabited the land and made it safe for the people before he retired to his Palace of the Waters.

When the people called him to protect them from Lai, an invader from the north, Lac Long captured, then married Lai's daughter (in some versions, Lai's wife), Au Co. From this union of Lac Long Quan, king of the race of dragons, and Au Co, queen of the race of fairies, came one hundred sons. Lac Long returned to the Kingdom of the Waters with fifty sons while Au Co moved to the mountains with the other fifty.*

When the sons reached manhood, one of their number was chosen king and named Hung, the first of the Hong Bang dynasty. Two more dynasties fol-

* P. J. Honey, *Genesis of a Tragedy: The Historical Background to the Vietnam War* (London: Ernest Benn, 1968), 1–6.

lowed before the Chinese conquered the people in
111 B.C., the year that saw the beginning of one
thousand years of Chinese rule. Vietnamese folklore
reflects the strong influence of this thousand-year
exposure to Chinese control and culture.

The thousand years under China also profoundly
influenced the life of the people. Before the Chinese
came, the people had been farming, fishing, and
hunting folk. The Chinese brought engineering
techniques for building new roads, harbors, military
fortifications, and water works, in addition to new
methods of rice planting and cultivation. They also
introduced writing skills and learning, and religion
and religious philosophies, notably Confucianism,
Buddhism, Taoism, and animism.

As did the Chinese and many other Southeast
Asians, the Vietnamese believed in the world of spirits. They believed that spirits inhabited animals,
nature, and the dead. Most important were the
ancestral or guardian spirits who were honored
through rituals in religious practice. Since the Vietnamese regarded their ancestors as protectors of
their families, they frequently addressed their ancestors through prayers in times of unusual fortune or
misfortune. An altar was set up in the family living
room where it served as a unifying force, a symbol of
family solidarity. Honoring one's forebears instilled
pride in the family and strengthened one's desire to
avoid offending them or soiling their reputations in
any way.

Like their ancestors, Vietnamese in the twentieth
century live by a set of clearly defined principles,
with the family as the hub around which all else
revolves. The family's welfare takes precedence

over individual interests and needs. Family loyalty and filial piety not only define an individual's role in relation to the immediate or extended family but also specify an individual's obligations to his or her ancestors.

Today's Vietnamese continue to value faithfulness, virtue, education, wisdom, intelligence, status, and harmony in personal relationships. In social contacts they prize good manners and tend to judge others by their use of courteous behavior.

The stories in this collection provide some insight into the rich history, culture, and religious beliefs of the Vietnamese. The tales are faithful to the originals from the North and South Vietnamese, from mountain tribes, from lowland farmers, and from fishing people.

The tales are varied in style and purpose. Some are mildly instructive while others are entertaining. Some reveal moral codes and values; some are humorous, poignant, and philosophical. They present historical legends and Buddhist didactic tales, tricksters and heroes, animals and magic, and the complexities of family and community relationships. All have something to say about human nature.

In earlier years, these stories were told and retold countless times. Each time the teller reworked his material artistically and adapted it to the circumstances of his audience. The stories were written down much later, and in their present form they have an enduring place in the literature of the Vietnamese. They supply a sense of cultural identity, and they also help explain the inexplicable, impart wisdom and insight, convey significant psychological and spiritual truths, provide models for an emerging spiritual idealism, and offer humorous relief from the harsh realities of life. The tales assume an international dimension as children and adults realize that people in other countries are reading similar stories in their own languages.

Concern is often expressed about themes of sexism and violence in folktales. Beliefs about women as passive, dependent persons represent views held not only by the Vietnamese, but also by many male-oriented cultures of years past, including Western cultures. The presence of violence in the form of murders and suicides in traditional stories is a reflection of the low value those early cultures placed on human lives. Suicides were common among many peoples, including the Vietnamese, as a means of proving innocence and avoiding disgrace. Learning about these aspects of earlier times can help young people develop a sense of perspective and can clarify and deepen the contemporary experience.

Vietnamese children today hear stories told in their homes by grandmothers or mothers. At school, teachers introduce tales to preserve the Vietnamese heritage and, occasionally, to coach the young in various forms of social behavior.

Typically the tales begin with the storyteller saying, *Hoi xua*, "One time in the past" or *Ngay xua*, "A long time ago." *Duoi thoi vua*, "Under the reign of King ____," introduces the historical tales.

The twenty-seven narratives here are arranged in four groups: Foibles of Man and Quirks of Animals; Tales from the Lowlands and the Highlands; Spirit World; and Food, Love, and Laughter. Brief notes after the stories offer historical and cultural background on the tales' themes, symbols, events, and characters. The stories are enhanced by the delicate brush, pen, and ink drawings of Janet Larsen.

Although this volume is intended for the general reader, beginning with children in the middle grades (5–8), it also provides a rich source for storytellers. The narratives, drawn from the careful translations of former residents of Vietnam, have been selected for their authenticity, their variety of content and style, and their appeal to American readers and listeners.

FOIBLES OF MAN
AND
QUIRKS OF ANIMALS

Under the Starfruit Tree

Once there were two brothers whose parents died. The parents left everything to their older son—everything, that is, but the starfruit tree, which they left to their younger son.

The older son lived very well in the large house that his parents had left him. He wore silk robes and hired workers to cultivate his fields so he did not have to soil his hands. He spent his time playing chess with his friends or listening to music. He seldom visited his younger brother, who was very poor, and all but forgot him.

The younger son had no place to live, so he built a shack under the starfruit tree. He dressed in rags, the only clothes he could afford. He spent his days taking care of his starfruit, pruning the tree when necessary, and clearing the fallen fruit and leaves from the ground. He sold his fruit at the market in the morning and from a stand under his tree in the afternoon. He barely managed to make a living.

One day, as he gathered the fallen leaves from under the tree, he heard a rush of air above him and saw a great shadow cast upon the ground. He looked up and saw an eagle circling overhead to perch on the highest branch of the starfruit tree. The whole

He spent his days taking care of his starfruit . . .

tree shivered under the large bird's weight. The eagle looked down over its beak at the astonished young man and said, "Boy, I crave some of your fruit."

"I do not mind if you help yourself," the young man said, "but since this is the only way I can keep alive, please leave some for me."

The eagle ate some of the fruit and flew away. It came again the next day, ate more fruit and left. This went on for several days.

Every day the young man looked anxiously at the diminishing supply of fruit left on the tree. One day, while the eagle was eating his fruit, the young man said, "Sir, tomorrow I shall have just enough to sell at the market."

"Very well, boy," the eagle answered. "Sew a sack and tomorrow place it under the tree."

The young man did as he was told. The next day the eagle swept down to the bag hanging from the tree trunk. The eagle coughed twice, dropped a bar of gold into the bag, and flew away without eating any fruit. The boy took the gold into town and bought everything he needed. He found that he could afford much more than he bought; he was wealthy now.

News of this sudden fortune reached the older brother's ears. He hurried to visit his brother, who still lived under the starfruit tree, and asked how true the story was. When his brother told him everything, the older brother offered to trade his home and all he owned for the starfruit tree. His brother agreed.

So the younger son now owned a large house in the village, fields with crops, and all the wealth the eagle had given him. He was most comfortable indeed.

The next day the older son sat under the tree and scanned the skies for the eagle. The eagle did not come that day. The young man was most upset. Neither did it come the following day. But on the third day, just as he was about to set off for the village to complain to his younger brother, he heard a great flapping of wings and saw the tree cast into the shadow of the eagle.

As the eagle swooped down to the tree, the young man shouted up to the bird, "If you want to eat the starfruit, you must give me something in return."

"Very well," the eagle said. "Tomorrow put a pouch under the tree."

The older brother was prepared with a very large bag that he promptly put under the tree. He waited impatiently for tomorrow. When the eagle returned the following day, the young man climbed the tree hastily and reached out to hold on to the eagle by clutching its legs. He wanted to be sure the eagle left the bar of gold before it flew away.

The eagle in turn grasped the young man in its claws, flapped its wings, and soared into the sky. It flew until they were over the ocean, where it released its hold on the older brother. Too late, the older brother learned that it really did not pay to be greedy.

"Under the Starfruit Tree" is a story from the peasant folk of Vietnam. Narrators could have used this story to warn against avarice and to teach that good actions should be the major concern of a person's life.

How the Tiger
Got Its Stripes

A long, long time ago tigers were green, yellow, reddish, or even white in color, but they had no stripes. They were one solid color.

One day, a sandy-colored tiger wandered into a rice field, looking for food. There he saw a huge water buffalo pulling a plow for a small man. The even color of the tiger's tawny coat blended into the sandy knoll where he crouched to view the scene below him. He twitched his tail as he watched the buffalo. Now and then the farmer flicked his switch on the buffalo's back, and the tiger saw the animal pull harder.

The tiger watched the buffalo straining and pulling and suffering. As the tiger grew hungrier, the buffalo looked more delicious. Finally the tiger strolled up to the water buffalo and stopped him.

"Why does a powerful animal like you allow a small, puny man like him to make you suffer?" he asked. "Why, you can pick him up and eat him, just as easily as I can eat you."

"This small creature," the buffalo said, "has the intelligence to make me work. That's why I submit to him."

"Intelligence?" the tiger asked. "What is *intelligence?*"

"I don't know, because I don't have it," the buffalo answered. "Ask the man."

Now the tiger was proud of being the most feared animal in the jungle; but he had never heard of this thing called *intelligence.* He looked at the small, skinny farmer and the huge water buffalo.

Intelligence, he reasoned, makes it possible for the man to control that huge creature. Ah, what he could do with that intelligence, he thought. He would never have to worry about his next meal.

The tiger had to find out what *intelligence* was. He approached the man.

"What is *intelligence?*" the tiger asked the man. "I want to see it."

"I can explain what it is, but I cannot show it to you," the man said. "I left it at home. If I go home to get it, you will eat my buffalo."

"I will not eat your animal," the tiger said. "I promise."

"I do not trust you. As soon as I turn my back, you will eat my buffalo."

"Then what can I do to convince you that I won't?"

"Let me tie you to a tree trunk while I go home to get my intelligence. When I come back, I shall untie you."

The tiger agreed to the farmer's plan and lay down by the tree. The man scratched his head as he looked at the tiger. "I cannot tie you if you lie down."

"Then do you want me to sit up?"

"Yes," the farmer said, "that is better. Now just hold the tree trunk with your legs. There!"

With the tiger standing up against the tree, the farmer tied him securely to the trunk. He left and soon returned with an armful of dry grass, which he left at the foot of the tree.

Then the man picked up his switch and began to beat the tiger. "This is my intelligence," he said. "And since you are so stupid, I will burn you and eat your meat."

He set fire to the dry grass. When the flames reached the tree, they scorched the rope that held the tiger. The tiger roared in pain. He struggled to break free and cursed himself for asking about *intelligence*. He shook off the last burning knot and, moaning, limped into the forest.

Ever since that day, tigers have dark stripes across their bodies from the burn marks left by the scorched rope.

"How the Tiger Got Its Stripes" is more than a simple *pourquoi* tale. The rural people of Vietnam, as in many agricultural areas, lived close to their animals, regarding them as essential coworkers. The water buffalo, introduced centuries ago by the Chinese, helped in many ways, especially in the cultivation of the rice paddies. Tigers, on the other hand, were greatly feared because they terrorized many villages. In this story, the quiet, industrious water buffalo remains true to its character and faithful to its master, while the tiger is outmaneuvered by a farmer's intelligence, thereby receiving its comeuppance.

Having been ruled hundreds of years by outsiders, the Vietnamese enjoy stories about the weak peasant's overcoming a powerful adversary through cleverness. This story reflects the light wit and scheming mind of the peasant who revels in happy endings.

The Jealous
Husband

Once, long, long ago, there was a young man named Truong Sinh. He was a very jealous husband. He followed his beautiful wife, Vu Thi, wherever she went. He prevented her from meeting people and questioned her about those times he was not with her. Vu Thi, who had come from a very poor family, never complained and remained a loving wife.

Soon after Truong Sinh and Vu Thi were married, Truong Sinh was drafted into the army and sent to war. The young couple bade a sad farewell. He left his ailing mother with Vu Thi, who was expecting their first baby. Six moons later, Vu Thi gave birth to a boy. She named him Dan. Before Dan was three moons old, Truong Sinh's mother became ill and died.

Vu Thi missed her husband very much. Daily she looked for him on the road leading to her home, but many moons went by, and he did not return. As Dan grew older, Vu Thi talked about his father every day and spoke happily of the time when he could be with them day and night.

When the war finally ended and Truong Sinh

came home, Dan was already three years old. Wanting to visit his mother's grave, Truong Sinh held out his hand to Dan and said, "Come, Dan, let us go and visit your grandmother's grave."

Dan cried and shook his head.

"Please do not cry," Truong Sinh said. "Daddy is very sad, too."

"Are you my daddy, too?" Dan asked. "You do not look like my other daddy who never spoke."

Truong Sinh was shocked. He questioned Dan closely.

"My daddy came every night," Dan said. "He followed mommy everywhere. When she sat down, he sat down. When she stood up, he stood up. But he never carried me."

Truong Sinh, whose jealous nature was never far below the surface, was angry. Instead of asking Vu Thi the truth about what Dan had told him, Truong Sinh began to insult her and criticize her.

Night after night she wept bitterly.

"Why are you so suspicious?" she asked. "When I went to the marketplace, I spoke to no one."

Truong Sinh would not reveal what Dan had told him.

One day Vu Thi could stand it no longer. She went down to the river and prayed to the River God. "If I have been faithful to my husband, please change me into a pearl in the water. If I have been an unfaithful wife, let the fishes eat me." Then Vu Thi jumped into the river.

When Truong Sinh discovered what had happened, he was deeply upset. He looked in vain for Vu Thi's body.

One sleepless night he sat beside the lamp and

tried to put Dan to sleep. The light from the lamp threw his shadow on the wall.

"Here is my dad!" Dan said, as he bowed to his father's shadow on the wall, the way his mother had taught him. Truong Sinh realized only then how wrong he had been.

Truong Sinh would never have seen Vu Thi again if not for a boatman from Vu Thi's former village. About the time Vu Thi disappeared in the river, this boatman dreamed that a girl in a blue dress asked him to save her. Early the next morning a fisherman offered him a turtle with a blue shell. Remembering his dream, he refused to eat the turtle and released it into the ocean. He then left for the sea in a fishing boat. A sudden storm at sea threw him overboard, washing his body ashore on an island. A sacred turtle dressed in rich robes came to revive him and led him to her palace in an underwater cave.

She told the boatman that she was the turtle with the blue shell. "Please accept my deepest gratitude," she said. "And now, I honor you with this banquet." She clapped her hands, and servants came running to lay the banquet table. Many beautiful women surrounded them. The boatman recognized one of them as Vu Thi.

Surprised, he asked Vu Thi, "Why are you here?"

"The gods took pity on me," she explained, "so when I cast myself into the river, they brought me here."

Before the boatman left the palace, Vu Thi gave him her hairpin, asking him to tell Truong Sinh that if he wanted to make up for his unfairness to her, he should build an altar on a floating raft on the river.

She promised to appear after he lighted a candle on the altar.

The boatman went home and relayed Vu Thi's message to the grieving Truong Sinh, who did not believe him until he saw the hairpin. He recognized it right away.

For three evenings, Truong Sinh held a ceremony on the river with lighted candles on an altar. On the third evening Vu Thi appeared, riding along the middle of the river in a flower carriage. With several other carriages following her and with flags flying in the breeze, she led a colorful parade.

Truong Sinh was overjoyed to see Vu Thi.

"Vu Thi!" he shouted. "I am here!" He waved his arms to make sure that she would see him.

"I thank you for coming to see me," Vu Thi called back, "but I cannot return to earth. Good-bye."

The carriages continued down the river, and the whole procession vanished.

Truong Sinh was very sad, but from that day on he resolved to devote his life to his small son.

"The Jealous Husband" belongs to a category of stories with a sophisticated moral.

War was a common condition throughout the long history of Vietnam. In this tale, Truong Sinh was gone for at least three years. The teachings of Confucius gave each person a strict code of behavior, spelling out, for example, the duties of a wife to her husband. The importance of honor and duty was so great that Truong Sinh's wife believed she must commit suicide to prove her innocence. The Vietnamese believe that because Vu Thi died of an injustice, her soul was very unhappy. Justice was restored when Truong Sinh held ceremonies with offerings and candles, allowing Vu Thi's soul finally to be at peace.

The Snake
Princess

Once, long ago, Do Sinh, a young man, stood watching a group of children shouting and dancing around a snake, teasing it with sticks and long branches. "Beat the snake!" "Turn it over!" "Make it curl into a ball!"

He saw that the snake was carrying unborn eggs in her body and was close to death from exhaustion. After watching for some time, he took pity on the snake and bought her from the children, then freed her.

Not long after that, a beautiful young woman came to visit him. "I am the daughter of the King of Snakes in the mountain of Nam Son," she said. "I am the snake you saved from the children's cruel teasing a few days ago."

"If you are the daughter of the King of Snakes," Do Sinh said, "then you belong to the snake family. How can you appear as a human being?"

"All animals, including snakes, can take the form of human beings if they know how to improve themselves. But human beings cannot take the form of animals," she said, "because they are the finest living things created by the gods. The gods want to keep them that way."

"I am glad of that," Do Sinh said. "I do not care to be an animal."

"I come today to return the favor and save your life," she said.

At this moment, two snakes crept down from the rafters, stood on their tails and greeted her by nodding their heads three times in the princess' direction and then nodding to Do Sinh when she commanded them to do so.

Three days before, Do Sinh had tried to kill a snake. It had run away, but today that snake had returned with its mate to take revenge on him.

"Forget your hatred for each other," the princess said. "Buddha taught us to forget revenge, not to dwell on it. Tell other snakes never to bother Do Sinh again."

As the two snakes bowed their way out, the princess turned to Do Sinh and said, "Before I leave, will you tell me if you have any other reason to hate snakes?"

"They are poisonous," Do Sinh said. "Two moons ago I lost my best friend because of a snake's bite."

"What about people?" she asked. "People are just as poisonous as snakes. Recall how much harm they do by what they say. They tell lies and hurt others so that people can even die as a result. Snakes are not the only ones who are poisonous."

"You are right," Do Sinh said. "I had never thought of it in that way." When he wanted to talk further, the princess said, "Today I must go, but I shall come again."

True to her promise, she returned again and again, each time bringing her equally beautiful younger sister with her. Many times, in their visits, Do Sinh forgot that they were really snakes, for they always appeared in human form. Eventually the King of Snakes sent a message to Do Sinh through his older daughter that he wanted Do Sinh to marry the younger princess.

Although Do Sinh no longer hated snakes and had come to regard both princesses as friends, he told the older sister, "I am honored, but I am a human being and cannot live with a snake."

"We can become human beings, like my sister and I are right now. We can live just the way you do," she said. "Remember what I said about animals improving themselves?"

So Do Sinh agreed to marry the snake princess who took the form of a woman. She lived with him as a human being. They lived happily in the mountains and raised a family.

Years later, after Do Sinh died, his children built an altar for him. At his death anniversary every year for many years, his descendants noticed the appearance of a long snake whose body curled around the incense burner.

"The Snake Princess" introduces the concept of *tu luyen*, by which humans and animals could improve themselves through training and meditation, preferably away from others. When an animal improved itself, it became a human being; a human being through meditation and study could become a better person.

It is not surprising that Do Sinh tried to kill a snake. Snakes were much feared and despised. In the olden days, Vietnam was so overrun by snakes that it was not uncommon to hear about people dying in their sleep after having been bitten by a snake. A person who destroyed snakes was considered a bene- factor. Many years ago a man named Hua Ton saved the popu- lation by learning the witchcraft of snake killing. When he died at the age of 130, he was thought to have flown into the sky with his family. Later he was consecrated by the king.

Mister Thirty

Long, long ago there was a young man who cared for his aging mother. Every night he set his home-made nets in a swiftly flowing river. Back he came early in the morning to gather the captured fish. In this way he put food on the table for his mother and himself.

One morning he came back to a torn net with not a single fish in it. After repairing his damaged net, he set his three nets as usual. The next morning all three nets were torn and empty. This happened for several days in succession, and the young man became more and more upset.

"I must stop this vandalism!" he said. "You are getting weaker without food, Mother. I will hide in a bush by the river tonight and catch the culprit."

The next morning, villagers found the young man's lifeless body on the river bank beside his torn nets.

"It is a tiger that killed him," one villager said.

"It must be a tiger," another agreed.

Soon everyone believed that a tiger had killed the young man, and all walked down forest paths in fear.

His mother was overcome with grief. She had lost her only son and her sole support. In her sorrow she

went to visit her son's grave every day. One afternoon she was so absorbed in her grief that darkness
fell before she realized the time. She began to walk
home as quickly as possible, then she saw a tiger.

"So," she said, forgetting fear because of her great
distress, "is it you who killed my son? Now there is
no one to support me. I shall die of loneliness and
hunger." The tiger stood there silently with his head
hung low. "Are you going to support me?" The tiger
began to nod. "Are you going to do for me what my
son did?" The tiger again nodded.

With tears in her eyes, the woman turned her
back on the tiger and slowly trudged home to an
empty house. The next day, and every fourth day
after that, she found a deer or wild hog laid at her
front door. She hungrily ate part of it and sold the
rest at the village market.

This went on for two moons before the old
woman decided to find out who was supporting her
so generously. She hid behind her door that night
and saw the same tiger she had seen by her son's
grave. He had come to deliver more freshly killed
game.

"So it is you," she said. "Please come in to visit
for a while."

Each time the tiger brought her food, she invited
him in. A warm friendship soon developed between
them.

One dark night he came to her with an arrow in
his shoulder. She tended him carefully and kept him
with her for several days until he was well enough to
go back to the forest.

This friendship continued until the old woman
lay dying. "Thank you for all your care of me," she

Is it you who killed my son?

said. "Please promise me never to kill people again." The tiger hung his head and nodded. He stayed quietly by her side till the end.

The following day villagers found wild game beside her front door. There was enough game to pay for a large funeral. On the night of the funeral, the forest was filled with the roar of a tiger.

"That is the tiger grieving for the old woman," the villagers said, nodding knowingly to each other.

For many years, on the thirtieth day of the last month of the year, when people waited with offerings for the spirits of their ancestors to come back to be with their families, the tiger returned with his offering of wild game.

"How loyal he is to the old woman!" the villagers said.

Stories about the steadfast loyalty of the tiger spread to other villages. It was not long before farmers and fishermen from different villages said, "Even if he is an animal, he is better than some people because he never forgets his offering on the thirtieth day of the last month of the year."

"Mister Thirty" is set in a time when tigers roamed the forests of Vietnam. Temples, built to worship them, each contained a picture of a white tiger surrounded by the green, the black, the yellow, and the reddish tigers. People were afraid to destroy tigers because they were known to seek revenge. So eager were the authorities to rid the country of these predators that they rewarded every person who killed a tiger. To prevent other tigers from avenging a fellow creature's death, the authorities also "punished" the hunter with thirty symbolic strokes.

Not all tigers, however, sought revenge. According to Vietnamese belief, the nature of the tiger was either cruel and revengeful or faithful and sentimental, like Mister Thirty.

Although it may seem strange to us that the elderly woman forgave the tiger believed to have killed her son, Buddha had told his followers not to dwell on revenge (see also "The Snake Princess").

A familiar saying about misbehavior is attributed to this story: "You are not as good as certain animals, for you do not behave like a proper human being."

Tam and Cam

I

A long time ago there was a girl named Tam. She, her mother, and her father were a happy family. When Tam was still a young girl, her mother became ill and died. Several lonely years followed for Tam and her father. Then her father married again. His second wife, Tam's stepmother, was jealous of the love between Tam and her father. She locked Tam in her room and complained to her husband that Tam was lazy, that she was never around when there was work to be done. She took the needle and thread away from Tam and then complained to her husband that Tam did not do any mending.

Before long, Tam's stepmother had a baby girl. She was named Cam. When Cam was just beginning to walk, their father died, leaving Tam with her stepmother and half sister Cam.

Tam worked hard at home. "Tam!" her step-mother called every morning. "Clean the kitchen floor before you leave for the fields. You must work in the east cornfields today."

Every day it was the same—work in the house as

well as in the fields. Dressed in rags all day long, Tam longed to have pretty clothes. She never complained because, if she did, she knew she would gain nothing but punishment.

Cam did not have to work so hard. The truth was, she never worked at all. Dressed in frivolous, brightly colored clothes, she played day after day with her pet cat or entertained her mother with endless chatter.

One day their mother said, "Tam! Cam! Go to the pond and catch some prawns for dinner. Take your own basket and fill it to the top." As soon as they reached the pond, Tam waded into the water and began to fill her basket. By afternoon her basket was brimful with plump prawns.

Cam played all day, picking flowers for her hair, plucking fruit to munch, and dancing and singing around the pond.

When Tam said, "Cam, you must start gathering the prawns," Cam turned a deaf ear.

When the sun was low in the sky and it was time to go home, Cam looked at her empty basket, then at Tam's.

"Tam," she said, "you have mud all over your clothes and hair and face. How upset Mother will be! Go and clean yourself in the river."

"Yes, I must wash," Tam said. "I will not be long."

When she came back, Tam found her sister gone and her own basket empty. There was no time to fill her basket, and Tam was afraid to go home. Upset, she sat down and wept.

As she sobbed, Tam became aware of a soft humming sound. Looking up, she found a circle of light before her. The light became brighter and brighter until it briefly blinded Tam. In that moment, a beautiful woman stepped out of the light. "Why are you crying?" the woman asked.

"I have no more time to catch prawns to fill my basket," Tam said. "Cam took everything I had."

"Look in the basket now," the woman said.

Tam looked again and saw a catfish.

"Take the fish home and raise it," the woman said. "Be sure to feed it every day with whatever food you eat. Do not worry about your mother. She is so pleased with Cam today that she will not scold you." With that, she disappeared. Tam believed that the beautiful woman was her fairy guardian.

Tam took the fish home and called it Bong. She left it in the well in the back yard and always remembered to save some of her supper for it. Bong thrived on her care and grew quickly.

Every evening at supper, Cam noticed that Tam did not finish her dinner but left the table with her bowl. One day, she decided to follow her. At the well she heard Tam call out,

> Bong, come here,
> Come and get your share.
> Whatever I have
> I share with you,
> Whatever you have
> You share with me.

Cam memorized Tam's call and hurried back to tell her mother. The next morning, while Tam worked in the fields, Cam and her mother went to the well and called Bong. When Bong answered, they caught the fish. They cooked it and ate it before Tam came home.

After supper Tam went to feed Bong, but there was no answer to her call. Alarmed, she ran around the well, calling Bong. When she saw drops of blood by the well, she guessed what had happened and wept. Then Tam heard the voice of her fairy guardian.

"What has upset you?" the fairy guardian asked, placing her hand lightly on Tam.

"It is Bong," Tam said. "Somebody ate Bong. Now I have nothing and no one."

"Look for Bong's bones," her fairy guardian said. "Put them in four small bottles. Then bury a bottle under each leg of your bed."

Tam looked all over but could not find the bones. A rooster strutted up to her and crowed, then clucked,

> Out of sight,
> Far from light,
> A cup of rice
> Will give you the prize.

After he had his cup of rice, the rooster led Tam to the tree growing behind the kitchen wall. He pecked and scratched at the ground where the roots ended until he uncovered some of Bong's bones. Tam finished digging up the bones and placed them in four bottles. She then buried a bottle under each leg of her bed as she had been instructed.

Spring breezes blew winter rains away, and all the villagers talked about the coming Spring Festival. They talked about nothing else, because this was the one event of the year at which people met the king and his court. Everyone attended.

"See my new dress," Cam said. "I am going to the fair; I will meet the king."

"I wish I had a new dress to wear to the Spring Festival," Tam said.

The day of the Spring Festival came. Even without a new dress, Tam was excited. Just before they left for the festival, her stepmother turned to Tam and said, "Before you go to the fair, there is one more task for you to finish; separate the husks from the grain." She gave Tam a large basket of grain with husks. "When you finish, you may go."

Her stepmother had added more husks to increase the work for Tam. As she separated the husks from the grain, Tam wiped the hot tears that kept falling. She did not hear her fairy guardian appear.

"What is wrong?" her fairy guardian asked.

"Today is the Spring Festival," Tam said. "But I must separate the husks from the grain before I can go. I will not reach the bottom of this basket until many days after the fair ends."

"Dry your tears. The sparrows will help you." She whispered to a sparrow hopping on the windowsill, and soon many sparrows flew into the room. They finished the task in a short time.

When Tam saw the empty basket, her heart was lifted in happiness. Then she looked at the rags she wore, and her eyes filled with tears again.

"Go and dig up the bottles containing the bones," her fairy guardian said.

Tam dug up the four bottles. They no longer contained bones. One bottle contained a pair of white silk shoes with toes turned up gracefully, like those worn only by the nobility. Precious gems embroidered on the shoes sparkled in the sunlight.

The second bottle contained a dark orange scarf for her hair and a green scarf for her waist. From the third bottle Tam pulled a pair of long-legged black pants, a light yellow blouse, and a peach-colored dress, all made of the finest silk.

"Do you see that small clay horse in the last bottle?" her fairy guardian asked. "Now take it out of the bottle and place it gently on the ground outside the door."

As soon as Tam put it down, it started to grow. It grew until it reached the size of a real, full-grown horse. The horse carried a very handsome saddle.

"The horse will take you to the Spring Festival," the fairy guardian said.

As Tam rode the horse and started off for the fair, her eyes sparkled with excitement. She was going to the fair, after all, she thought, dressed in fine silks and riding a magnificent horse!

As she approached the fairgrounds, Tam's horse stumbled through a muddy puddle, causing one of Tam's shoes to slip off. She got off the horse to look for it.

While she was searching by the roadside, the king came down the same road on an elephant. The elephant stopped near the muddy puddle. It trumpeted once then refused to take a step forward. The king demanded to know why, and the guards were quick to investigate. They looked around the bushes and trees beside the road. One of them found Tam's dainty white shoe, unsoiled by the mud around it. He picked it up and showed it to the king.

"Such a small and exquisite shoe!" the king

exclaimed. "It must belong to someone beautiful."
The more he gazed at the shoe, the more he fell
under its spell.

He was so bewitched that he wanted to meet the
owner of the shoe without delay. He ordered all the
women and girls to come and try the shoe. Whom-
ever the shoe fit, he proclaimed, would become his
wife. All the girls and women at the fair tried the
shoe—even Cam and her mother attempted to pull
it on. When Tam's turn came to try it, Cam whispered to her mother, "That girl looks like Tam."

"Impossible," her mother said. "She couldn't
have finished her work yet. And pray tell, where
would she get such beautiful clothes?"

The shoe fit Tam. True to his word, the king took
her to his palace to marry her. As she left to go, Tam
caught sight of Cam and her stepmother standing
there with disbelief in their eyes. She smiled and
waved to them as the king's procession carried her
along to the palace, where she and the king were
happily married.

II

Cam and her mother did not have a chance to ask
Tam how she had acquired her beautiful clothes for
the Spring Festival until later that year when she
came home for her father's death anniversary. They
were very, very jealous of Tam's good fortune. But
when she came home, they hid their jealousy and
pretended they were happy to see her.

"Tam, dear," her stepmother said, "it is so good to
have you home again. Will you pick a betel nut for

the altar? I am sure your father would be happy to know that you picked it with your own hands."

"Of course, Mother," Tam said. Since the nut grew near the top of the tree, she had to climb quite high. When she was more than halfway to the top, the tree began to shake.

"What is happening?" Tam asked. "I feel the tree shaking."

"Dear Tam," Cam said, "there are so many ants on the trunk, I am trying to shake them loose." But Cam was really trying to saw through the trunk. Before Tam could pick the nut, she fell down with the tree and died.

Her stepmother then took Tam's clothes and dressed Cam in them. She sent Cam to the palace in her sister's place. Cam told the king, "Tam became ill and died, so I am taking her place." The king believed her and the whole palace welcomed Cam. Very soon the king found that Cam did not please him. She was not gentle. She was lazy, and she thought only of her own comfort. He missed Tam more and more.

Tam's soul, meanwhile, could not rest in peace, because death had been so sudden and unexpected. Her soul took the form of a canary. She flew to the palace and, chattering cheerfully, followed the king wherever he went. One day he said, "You remind me of Tam. If you are my wife's spirit, come into the sleeve of my robe." He then lifted his arms, which opened his wide sleeves. The canary flew into his right sleeve. Then, fearing for her safety, the king put the bird into a beautiful cage and took her wherever he went. He talked to her as if she were Tam in person. Even when asleep, he kept her next to him.

Once a day he opened the door to the cage to let her fly free.

Cam did not know of the canary until one day, while she supervised the laundering of the king's clothes, the canary flew by and sang,

> If you wash my husband's clothing,
> Wash it clean,
> Wash it clean.

Cam knew right away that the canary was Tam's soul. She was afraid but, at the same time, angry at Tam for taunting her. She began to think of ways to get rid of the bird, but she could not get her hands on it. She frowned and chewed on her lower lip as she wondered what to do. Finally she decided to visit her mother to ask her advice.

"As soon as the king lets her out of his sight," her mother said, "catch her and kill her. Then cook her and give her to the cat. Bury the feathers so she won't have a body to come back to."

Cam went back to the palace. She bribed a guard to get her the cage while the king was at a meeting with his advisers. She followed her mother's advice and killed the canary, cooked her, fed her to the cat, and buried the feathers in the courtyard.

Soon after, a tree grew on the spot where she had buried the feathers. It grew quickly into a beautiful tree. The king noticed it and decided to tie a hammock to the branches so he could rest there in the afternoons. Whenever he went to the hammock to lie down, he felt that Tam was with him, and he felt peaceful and relaxed.

Cam was jealous of all the time the king spent

under the tree. While he was out one afternoon, she ordered a guard to chop down the tree. She instructed the court carpenter to make a loom from the wood.

Whenever she used the loom, she heard,

> You tried and tried,
> You have my husband.
> Revenge is what
> I will have.

Cam was afraid. She quickly stored the loom and allowed no one to touch it. Again in a predicament, she frowned and chewed on her lower lip, wondering what to do. She decided to visit her mother for advice.

"Burn it," her mother said. "Bury the ashes far away from the palace."

Cam went back to the palace. She followed her mother's advice and burned the loom, then buried the ashes far, far away.

Soon after, a tree grew from the ashes. The tree was covered with many flowers but bore just one small fruit at its top. The yellow fruit gave off a beautiful aroma.

An old woman from a nearby village passed it every day on her way to her roadside tea shop and, each time, stopped to admire it. She noticed, too, that the fruit had ripened but remained on the tree. One day she stood under the tree and said, "You are such a beautiful fruit, I want to take you home to smell and admire. I will never eat you. If you are going to fall, let me have you to put on my table."

As soon as she said that, the fruit fell into her bag.

Very happily, the old woman took it home. She placed it on the table and talked to it every day. She always told the fruit when she was leaving the house, where she was going, and what she planned to do.

After a few days, the woman came back from her shop to find her house cleaned, the laundry done, and her dinner prepared and on the table. This happened every day and the old woman was puzzled. So, one morning, pretending to go out, she hid behind the door. She saw a beautiful young woman step out of the fruit. The old woman rushed in and grabbed her, at the same time smashing the fruit.

From that day, Tam, for it was she, stayed with the woman as her daughter. Tam helped her at home as well as at her little roadside shop.

The king and his court chanced to come by one day and saw the small, clean shop. He sat down to have some tea and a plate of betel nuts. The nuts were wrapped in the special way Tam had always wrapped the nuts for him.

"Who wrapped the leaves around the nuts?" he asked.

"My daughter," the old woman said.

"May I meet her?" the king asked. His surprise and happiness at seeing Tam again knew no bounds!

Cam, however, had a very unpleasant surprise when they returned to the palace. Tam was gentle to her as she had always been and did not appear to be angry at all. She looked so beautiful that Cam could not help asking, "How is it that your skin is so clear? How do you keep yourself looking so young?"

"If you want to know," Tam said, "I will tell you my secret. Dig a very deep hole in the ground and sit in it. Have someone pour water over you. Start with cool water and make it warmer and warmer in order to rejuvenate the skin."

Cam dug a deep hole. She sat down in it with a mirror in one hand. She shouted up to the servant who was pouring the water to make it hotter and hotter. She kept looking in the mirror to see if she looked younger. Before she could see any change, the water had become so hot it burned her skin, and she died.

When her mother heard the news, she hurried to the palace, leaned far over the edge to look, and fainted into the hole. She also died.

Then, and only then, was Tam free. Ever after, Tam and the king lived happily together in a long and peaceful life.

"Tam and Cam" reveals Confucian ethics, with its emphasis on rewarding good behavior and punishing bad behavior. Deceit, treachery, and greed are dealt with firmly in this story's intriguing twists. Buddhist beliefs in spirits and reincarnation are also present. Customs of the people are represented in the younger sister's taking Tam's place at the palace after her death.

The significance of colors in the lives of the people is woven into the tale. A woman wore her hair long and always tied it in a colored scarf. The color of the head scarf and that tied around the waist indicated noble or peasant rank. The fairy dressed Tam in yellow and orange, royal colors, appropriate for the daughter of a mandarin.

TALES FROM
THE LOWLANDS
AND THE HIGHLANDS

The Da Trang
Crab

Have you ever been to the seashore in the morning and seen tiny sand-colored crabs scurry from hole to hole? These are known as the Da Trang crabs, named after a hunter.

Da Trang, the hunter, lived in a time that is now long, long past. He hunted in the morning and, if he had a good day, came back with game in the afternoon. Every day on his way to the hunting grounds he passed a shrine in which he saw two spotted snakes curled up next to each other. He hated and feared snakes and often thought of killing them. But, as time passed and these snakes never bothered him, he began to leave game for them.

When he passed the shrine one day, he saw a strange, huge snake fighting with the two familiar spotted snakes. He took his bow and arrow and wounded the unusually large snake. It slithered away with one of the smaller snakes in pursuit. The other spotted snake was fatally wounded in the fight. Full of pity, Da Trang buried it.

That night in his sleep Da Trang received a visit from the surviving snake. It thanked the hunter for being kind to the two snakes and for burying its mate.

"In gratitude," it said, "I give you this pearl that

you must promise to keep with you always." So saying, it spit out a small pearl.

Da Trang woke up and found a beautiful pearl on
his pillow. He placed it in his mouth for safe-
keeping.

A few days later, while walking through the forest
to his hunting grounds, he heard two crows talking
to each other. The first one said, "Did you see the
wild pig by the stream?"

The second crow said, "Yes. Isn't it foolish to
doze in the open under the tree?" Da Trang was
amazed that he understood what the crows were
saying. When he asked them in what direction the
pig had gone, he found that they understood him,
too! Now he knew the magic of the pearl.

One of the crows offered to lead him to his prey.

"For leading me to such a fine catch," Da Trang
asked, "what can I give you in return?"

"Just leave me something to eat," the crow said.
"The insides of the pig will be enough for me."

With the crow directing him to good hunting
grounds and Da Trang leaving food for the crow, the
two worked well together. But one day an animal ate
the food left for the crow. The crow became very
upset and asked Da Trang why nothing had been
left.

"I left the entrails of the deer," Da Trang said.

"I do not believe you," the crow replied. "There
was nothing. Nothing! Not even a scrap!"

"I tell you, I left the promised portion for you."

"You are lying. If you do not keep your promise,
our bargain is off."

Both Da Trang and the crow were so angry that
the argument quickly built to a point where the

hunter took his bow and arrow and shot the crow. The crow caught the arrow in its claw and screamed its revenge.

Five days later a man's body, shot by Da Trang's poisoned arrow, was found in the river. Da Trang insisted that he was innocent, that the crow had done it. No one believed him. The magistrate threw him into jail.

Day after day Da Trang languished in prison, but the pearl made it possible for him to carry on conversations with the ants. The prison guards thought he was mad because, even though no one was around, Da Trang kept talking. Once he heard two rats discussing the king's warehouse of grain.

"It is so poorly protected," one rat said.

"How fortunate for us," the other replied. "It is so easy to steal the grain."

Da Trang called the guard and related this information to him.

"The king must be informed of this theft," he said.

The guard refused. "Why should I be punished for you?" he said. "I take a risk by repeating information given to me by a crazy man."

"If I am proved wrong," Da Trang answered, "I'll gladly take the punishment in your place."

So the guard relayed the information to the king, who found that he really was losing much of his grain.

The following week Da Trang saw a parade of ants hurrying by with food on their shoulders.

"Where are you going?" he asked.

"A big flood is coming," the ant said, "and we must move to higher ground."

Da Trang told the guard to pass on the warning. This time, without question, the guard let the king know immediately. The king moved everyone to higher ground—and none too soon—for three days later the biggest flood ever swept across the land.

The king was so impressed that he released Da Trang from prison and appointed him his adviser. The king took Da Trang and his pearl all over the country and was able to help many people by passing on information from birds and animals. This caused the people to love their king and the king to favor Da Trang.

One day the king wanted to listen to the fishes. He and Da Trang sailed out into the bay until they saw some squids. The squids were singing. Da Trang had never heard squids sing, and he thought it was so funny that he laughed out loud. Alas, the pearl fell out of his mouth and into the water.

The king ordered his men to dive into the water to look for it. For days they searched in the water and the sand. Finally everyone gave up the search.

Da Trang begged the king to fill the ocean with sand so he could look for his magic pearl. When the king refused, Da Trang was very upset but continued to dig in the sand at the seashore. He spent the rest of his life sifting through handfuls of sand. He even asked the king to bury him on the beach when he died because he planned to continue his search after death.

Da Trang died an unhappy and dissatisfied man.

Months later, people found a small crab coming out of a tiny hole in the sand, creating little mounds that were quickly washed away by waves. People shook their heads and whispered, "Da Trang's restless soul has taken the form of a sand crab that turns over every grain of sand in an endless search for the magic pearl. How futile."

"The Da Trang Crab" reflects the Buddhist belief in reincarnation. Today this story is remembered in a Vietnamese proverb that says a person who pursues an impossible task, forgetting the limits of his or her own abilities, is like the Da Trang crab.

The
Scholar Be

The gods love virtue, or goodness of character. They often protect and help a virtuous man, a man such as the scholar Be.

Do Be was a student poor in wealth but rich in honesty and integrity. When he completed his studies, he had a long way to travel to the city of Thang Long where the examinations were being given. Because he was so poor, he first had to work to save enough money for the trip.

On the road to Thang Long, he passed a small temple and came to a tiny tea shop nearby. The woman who served his tea had seen him coming. "When you pass in front of a temple," she said, "you must do *ha ma* (get off your horse and pay your respects to the god of the temple). If you do not do this, the god of the temple will punish you." Do Be did not believe her.

When he left the tea shop, he heard the sound of someone walking behind him. He turned around to see a man who looked like a scholar. Do Be was not aware that this was the god of the temple, who wanted to know why Do Be did not do *ha ma*. In order to find out, the god had to appear in the form of a human being.

"Are you going to take the examinations, too?" he asked Do Be. When Do Be said yes, the god said, "Let us go together." As they walked, he said, "You did not do *ha ma* before the temple. Why is that?"

"I was walking and had no horse," Do Be replied, "so how could I get off the horse? I did not take my hat off because the sun is very hot. Why should I take my hat off and bow? I need no pardon; I'm a good person."

"You mean you are a very honest person?" the god asked.

"No, I did not say I was; but then, I never tell a lie and never break a law."

The proud little god was offended. Because Do Be did not do *ha ma*, the god felt that the scholar was irreverent. The god wanted to punish Do Be, but, first, he vowed to catch him in a lie or a dishonest deed.

So the two continued on their journey to Thang Long. Do Be, of course, was completely ignorant of his companion's intentions and godly powers.

As the sun rose in the sky, Do Be became increasingly thirsty. "I am thirsty," he said. "I wish I had something to drink." Through the god's power, Do Be saw a field of sugarcane. He called for the owner, but no one appeared.

"Go ahead and take some sugarcane to chew," the god said. "No one is around so no one will know."

"There are thousands and thousands of sugarcane plants, but it is not right to take one," Do Be said. "Somebody planted each of the thousands and somebody has been taking care of them. I shall eat two stalks and leave the owner something." He chewed two stalks of sugarcane and left sixteen *xu* saying, "When I left my home, each stalk cost six *xu*. I will pay eight *xu* each so that I will not take advantage of the owner."

Thwarted, the god planned more mischief.

Soon they came upon a field of ripe watermelons. To Do Be's eyes, every melon looked big and bursting with juicy sweetness.

"Oh, look," the god said, tempting Do Be again. "The watermelons look so sweet. Aren't you hungry now?"

Do Be's mouth watered as he gazed longingly at the watermelons. How refreshing just one bite would be! But he turned away and said, "No, I must save what little money I have for the trip."

The god silently cursed in frustration.

Soon they came to an inn where the god suggested they spend the night. Two pretty young women came out to greet them. Fluttering their fans teasingly, they invited the men in.

"Who is the owner of this inn? May I speak to him?" Do Be asked.

"No one's here but us," the girls said. "Come in and stay the night." Each girl took an arm and urged Do Be into the inn.

"No," Do Be said, releasing their hands, "it is wrong for a young unmarried man to sleep in the same room with a pretty girl. We had better go on."

So they continued on their way while the god fumed to himself.

They soon came to a well. Do Be borrowed a pail to draw water from the well to quench their thirst. Instead of just water, the pail came up with gold and water.

"What luck!" the god said. "Take it! Take it! It's

all yours. You can use it for the rest of the trip and in the capital city."

"This gold floats on the water," Do Be said. "Human gold would be at the bottom. This must belong to some god."

As he was about to pour all the gold back into the well, a gold serpent jumped from the pail into the well.

When they finally reached their destination, the god wanted to show Do Be the city, knowing that this was his first time in Thang Long. As they walked in the famous city, Do Be appeared to recognize all the important sights. He did not show any surprise, nor did he marvel at the beautiful buildings.

"You have been here before!" the god said. "You lied to me."

"No, I did not lie," Do Be said. "I have read many books about these buildings and places. This is the first time I am seeing them and I am excited. But, you know, they are just as I had expected."

The god now began to doubt his own feelings of ill will.

They stayed at an inn with other scholars who were taking the examinations. Do Be heard a great deal of talk, especially about the chairman of the examinations, who liked to be bribed. If a scholar did not bribe him, so the gossip went, he was almost sure to be failed. The scholars were all abuzz with this rumor, but Do Be refused to believe it.

"It is only hearsay," he said. "The emperor would not send anyone dishonest to represent him."

"I will give you half of my gold," the god said, sincerely wanting to help Do Be, "so you can bribe the chairman." Do Be refused, insisting that he would pass solely on his ability.

By this time, the god's anger was gone. He began to admire Do Be's honesty and wanted to help him instead of destroy him. So when the chairman read Do Be's examination papers and, in spite of the excellent answers, decided to write *Poor* because Do Be had not given him a bribe, the god, through his magical powers, made the chairman write *Excellent*.

Do Be, as First Laureate, received a costume and hat from the emperor. As he began the trip back to his village, he thought happily of the celebration the villagers were planning for him. He recognized the same temple he had passed going in the other direction. The god of the temple was there, waiting to congratulate him.

"When I first joined you on your journey to Thang Long," the god said, "I was angry that you did not do *ha ma* and meant to punish you as soon as I caught you in a lie."

"I had no idea I had insulted you," Do Be said. "I did not mean to, and I apologize."

The god went on to describe how he had placed the temptations in Do Be's path and how he had made the chairman write *Excellent* instead of *Poor*.

"I have come to admire you and wish to be your friend from now on," he said.

The god's confession caused Do Be to believe that he had passed the examinations because of the god's help and not because of his own ability. Upon arrival in his village, he agreed to be in the parade but refused to be called First Laureate. He wrote to the emperor, explained the god's part in his examinations, and petitioned the emperor to cancel his graduation.

When the emperor read the letter, he immediately ordered someone from the Academy of Letters to reread Do Be's examination papers. The papers were judged excellent. The emperor requested Do Be's presence at court. Do Be appeared in his poor peasant clothes with no shoes on his feet.

Amazed at the sight, the emperor asked, "What happened to the costume of First Laureate?"

"I do not deserve to be First Laureate," Do Be answered. "I plan to return the costume to you."

"The chairman of the Academy of Letters read your examination papers. He tells me they are excellent. You deserve the title."

To celebrate this occasion, the emperor honored Do Be at a banquet attended by the empress and the princesses. The empress urged a great deal of wine on Do Be, so he talked more than usual and disclosed the chairman's bribes. The next day the emperor demoted the chairman to the rank of teacher.

The following year when Do Be went to take the next level of examinations, he went by the same temple. This time not only was Do Be riding a horse, but he also did *ha ma*, because he held the god of the temple in friendship and respect.

Do Be passed the examinations and became Trang Nguyen, a mandarin.

The god of the small temple, now very fond of Do Be, came to celebrate this event. He gave Be a diamond ring as a gift. It was a special ring that turned dull when a person told the wearer a lie and bright when the wearer was told the truth. The ring flew away if the wearer told the lie.

To test the ring, the emperor borrowed it and asked one of the laureates if he were married. This laureate said No, although he was married. Be's diamond turned dull. The emperor asked Be if he were married. The answer was No, and the diamond shone.

This intrigued the princesses, and they all wanted to see the ring. The emperor allowed them to do so only if they said they never told a lie.

Each princess said she never lied, and each time the ring lost its sparkle. One of the princesses, Lien Huong, corrected herself and said, "In my life I have lied a few times, but my lies were harmless because they were told in sympathy and kindness." With this, the diamond shone.

Princess Lien Huong so impressed Be that he offered her the ring. The emperor accepted it for her, then told Lien Huong that she must give Be a gift in return. She gave him a scarf that she herself had embroidered.

Before many moons, Do Be, the poor peasant boy who had struggled to afford a trip to the city and had appeared in the royal court in peasant clothing with no shoes, married the Princess Lien Huong—all because the gods smile on a virtuous man.

"The Scholar Be" centers around the taking of the mandarin examinations, a practice introduced by the Chinese during their thousand-year rule of Vietnam. To become a mandarin, or civil service official, one had to compete in public examinations at different levels. The examinations were open to all, rich and poor. Though a peasant, as in "The Scholar Be," could become a mandarin, he seldom did. These examinations required knowledge of Confucian doctrine and Chinese classics, as well as excellence in literary composition, particularly the writing of poetry. Usually only the wealthy had time for these pursuits.

The serpent is a symbol of wickedness and harm. If Do Be had touched the gold coins, the serpent would have bitten him.

The capital city of Thang Long has been renamed Hanoi.

A War
between Gods

During the reign of Hung Vuong XVIII, gods lived on this earth in harmony with men. Two gods who were well known to men were Son Tinh and Thuy Tinh.

Young, handsome Son Tinh, God of the Mountain, was loved for his good nature and affection for all living creatures. As he strolled along the beach one day, he was drawn to a boat that had just landed. He heard all six fishermen in the boat talking excitedly.

"Ha! Look at the size of this fish," shouted one of the fishermen, wearing a huge grin.

"How beautiful and unusual!" another said, with wonder in his voice.

"*Ua!* Think of the price we can get at the market."

"Let us cut it up right now while it is fresh," said another as he rubbed his hands together.

"This must be especially delicious," another said as he looked greedily at the fish.

"*Vay*, this one fish will pay us well for today's work."

All of these exclamations aroused Son Tinh's curiosity. "Let me see such a wondrous fish," he said, stepping into the boat. Surely, this was an extraordinary fish, he thought. It was unusually large and fleshy. Its colors changed from blue to green to the darkness of the deepest ocean. As Son Tinh marveled at the changing colors, he became aware of the fish's pleading eyes.

"This is no ordinary fish," he said. "You must not kill it. Let it go back into the ocean."

"No! We cannot do that. We must sell this fish," the fishermen cried out to Son Tinh.

"Then let me buy it from you," he said. "And I will pay you to take me out on the ocean to the spot where you caught it."

As soon as he released the fish into the sea, it leaped out of the water three times.

"Look," one of the fishermen said, pointing to the fish, "it is trying to thank you."

That night, as Son Tinh relaxed in his home on Mount Ba Vi, a tall good-looking young man called on him. His name was Thuy Tinh, God of the Water, whose kingdom was the ocean.

"Today," he said, "I took the form of a fish and went swimming. While I was a fish, I was without my magical powers. The fishermen caught me. If not for you, I would be dead, and I am deeply grateful. Please come with me to visit my city at the bottom of the sea."

Son Tinh was amazed at the wealth of Thuy Tinh's kingdom. "My own mountain kingdom does not have such riches and luxury," he said.

"Please," replied the grateful God of Water, "take whatever you want. It is small payment for saving my life."

"No," Son Tinh said. "I am happy with my own possessions and do not covet yours."

"Then please accept this," Thuy Tinh said, giving Son Tinh a well-worn book. "It is a book I inherited from my father." Just to please him, Son Tinh took the book and tucked it into his pocket. After he returned to his mountain kingdom, he examined it closely. Its script was very old. Upon reading it, he found it to be valuable, because it held the magical power to make all wishes come true.

"This is a marvelous book to own, a real Book of Wishes," he thought, "but I have everything I want and wish for nothing more." With that thought, Son Tinh carelessly pushed the book aside. He forgot all about it until the day King Hung Vuong announced a contest among gods and men for the hand of his daughter, the beautiful Princess My Nuong. Her beauty was so great that Son Tinh's scorn for possessions vanished.

He journeyed to the king's palace, just as hundreds of other hopeful suitors did. All but two failed to pass the contest. One was Son Tinh. The other was Thuy Tinh.

The king thought long and hard about these two gods. Each was equally suited to be husband to the sought-after princess. Finally the king decided to set them a task to complete. Each had to find and bring to him ten white elephants, ten giant tunas, ten tigers, ten sailfish, ten hundred-meter tall trees, and ten green pearls. Half of these were from Son Tinh's kingdom and the other half from Thuy Tinh's kingdom. Whoever brought these gifts to the king first would be the winner.

Son Tinh remembered his Book of Wishes. He went home and wished for everything that the king had requested. The next day he presented his gifts at the royal court and won the hand of Princess My Nuong.

Thuy Tinh, meanwhile, took two days to gather all the gifts, thus losing the princess. So much did Thuy Tinh want the beautiful princess that he was furious. Forgetting his friendship for Son Tinh, Thuy Tinh used all his godly powers to attack him. He corralled the waters from the sky and the ocean and raised the water level to the top of the mountain. Son Tinh easily kept his mountain home beyond the water's reach.

Again, beginning in the middle of the next moon calendar year and continuing for several moons, Thuy Tinh attacked the mountains with strong winds and rising waters. He continued to do this every year. Although he has not succeeded to this day, each year he tries to take the princess from Son Tinh by causing monsoons.

These monsoons, with wind, rain, and floods, take the people's homes, their crops, and even their lives. Each monsoon reminds the people of the continuing feud between Son Tinh and Thuy Tinh, the two warring gods.

"A War between Gods" is set in the reign of the last emperor of the first royal dynasty of Vietnam, believed to be around the third century B.C. This is a famous legend relating the story of the confrontation between the Mountain Spirit (Son Tinh) and the Water Spirit (Thuy Tinh). Son Tinh, a son of Lac Long Quan and Au Co, is said to have followed his father to the sea but later returned to dwell on Mount Tan Vien, the Olympus of Vietnamese mythology.

Believing that all things had spirits and personalities, the people of Vietnam used this tale to explain the annual occurrence of torrential rains, the monsoons.

How the Dao People
Came to Be

There once was a man who decided he wanted to eat the Thunder God. First he had to catch him.

He thought of a plan to trap the god, and he asked his two sons to help. They spread water buffalo manure all over the mud walls and roof of their house, except for a spot on the roof where the man could sit and wait with his bucket drum and torch.

Night came, followed closely by a storm with lightning, thunder, and wind but no rain. The man beat on his drum and swung the torch to attract the awesome Thunder God. The god looked down from his dark clouds and roared, "Who is causing that noise!" Thunder rolled in answer, "A man on earth wants to eat your flesh."

"I will teach this fool a lesson," the god said, and he jumped on the roof to strike the man. But, of course, he slipped on the manure and slid down the side of the house right into a bag held by the two sons.

The man and his sons dragged the heavy bag across the courtyard to a storage room in the house. They let the god out of the bag and into the storage room and bolted the door. The man then warned his

He slipped on the manure and slid down the side of the house . .

sons to guard the room. "Do not give him any water," he added. "I am going to the market to buy some salt to flavor his flesh."

The fierce god bellowed in frustration from his prison and the two boys quaked at the ear-splitting thunder.

But while the man was gone, the god softened his voice and asked the brothers what they were called, how old they were, and what they did every day. The god's thunderous voice frightened the boys, but they answered his questions and soon found themselves describing one of their favorite games.

"My eyes can see through the wall," the god said, "so play it outside this door."

The two boys drew two straight lines a handspan apart on the ground. Then they drew two other lines, also a handspan apart, which crossed the first two lines, thus creating one closed and eight open cells. Taking turns, each boy tried to be first to place beans in three cells in a straight line. The Thunder God roared with laughter. "Well done!" he said. "Play again!"

After a while, the Thunder God said, "All this fun makes me thirsty. Bring me some water to drink!"

By then, the boys were having so much fun that they forgot their father's instructions and promptly obeyed the Thunder God. As they unbolted the door to hand him the water, they had a good look at the fiercely muscular, barrel-chested being who was the God of Thunder. With nostrils streaking flashes of lightning, the Thunder God was indeed a sight to terrify two young boys.

Instead of drinking the water, the god threw it at the roof. Where the water touched, the roof softened and fell, leaving an opening to the sky. The god pulled out a tooth and gave it to the boys, telling them to bury it to use later when danger threatened. Then he flew through the roof.

The two brothers buried the tooth in the soil. The tooth immediately grew into a vine with an enormous orange squash. Meanwhile the thunderstorm continued. But now the rains came down in a deluge, with thunder, wind, and lightning. It rained so much that, in no time at all, the storm caused a great flood that swept away all the people and all the houses in the world.

When the two brothers found the waters rising, they cut a door around the stem end of the big orange squash and climbed in for shelter. Throughout the rain, the huge squash bobbed and floated on the water with the boys inside.

The boys' father was also caught in the flood. He opened his umbrella and climbed into it to float on the water. The water rose so high that the umbrella bumped the door to the Thunder God's house.

"Oh, no!" the god said, when he saw who was at the door. "You are the man who wanted to eat my flesh."

"I still do," the man said.

"Wind!" the Thunder God called. "Blow him to the moon." And as quick as a clap of thunder, the god stopped the rain. Just as quickly, the man found himself on the moon, his umbrella handle tangled in the branches of a banyan tree.

When the flood subsided, the boys came out of the squash and found they were the only people left on earth. They sowed the seeds of the squash all over the highlands. These seeds became the Dao people.

Today, when the Dao people look up at the moon, they see a man sitting at the foot of a banyan tree.

"How the Dao People Came to Be" is a tale told by the Dao, who live in the uplands of North Vietnam. Geographically, Vietnam is divided into two distinct parts: the low-lying areas along the coastline, including the deltas and cities; and the mountain areas. People living in the mountains, called the highlanders, belong to different tribes; they are not considered to be ethnic Vietnamese.

The Dao people are highlanders and, like most other highlanders, belong to an ethnic minority group. Until recently, these highlanders have stayed in the mountains within their own villages, mingling little with other highlanders and almost never with the lowlanders. Consequently, through the centuries, they have developed beliefs that are different from those held by the Vietnamese. The Vietnamese, in turn, have been slow in accepting the highlanders and their culture.

In this story, the Dao people explain not only where they came from but also what they see in the moon. Because the moon appears to all mankind and furnishes a common object of interest everywhere, many cultures, including that of the Dao, tell stories about who the "man in the moon" is and how he came to be there.

The Worm
and the Snail

In the hills of Vietnam, there lived a family with
two daughters. Every day the two sisters went to the
fields to cut grass for their pigs to eat and to the forest to gather wood for fire. On the way home from
work one day, the two girls ate some figs. That evening, they felt very strange.

In time, the two sisters gave birth, one to a green
worm and the other to a snail. As soon as they saw
their babies, the two new mothers fainted. The
women who had helped at the birthing ran from the
room and out to the streets, screaming, "Demon!
Demon!"

Their mothers and all the villagers were frightened and truly believed that the worm and the snail
were demons. Everyone, including the two new
mothers, ran away, leaving the two little creatures
by themselves in the deserted village.

For many years the worm lived on one side of the
village, and the snail lived on the other. They nodded and smiled and greeted each other with a "Good
day," but they hardly spoke.

One day while the worm was eating his noonday
meal, he felt very lonely. He wanted to talk to someone. He visited the snail, who was slowly inching
her way home with twigs for firewood. The worm

The snail was slowly inching her way home with twigs for firewood.

greeted the snail and said, "Since we are each alone, why do we not live together?"

"Yes! Oh, yes!" the snail said. "I will be glad to have company. I find I am talking to myself in the evenings. That is when I get terribly lonely."

So the worm and the snail became husband and wife.

Before many moons had passed, a torrential rain awakened them in the middle of the night. It swirled around their house in the strangest way.

The following afternoon, while the snail was hustling about in the kitchen, she happened to look up to see a handsome man standing in the doorway. Surprised, she asked, "Who are you?"

"I am your husband," he said. To prove it, he threw his dry, shriveled worm skin at her feet.

That same evening, while the husband lay relaxing in his hammock, a beautiful woman with a vessel of water walked into his courtyard.

"My wife is not here," he said. "She is down at the stream."

The woman thrust a snail shell at him. "I *am* your wife," she said.

They looked at each other and decided that the strange rainfall of the night before had caused them to become human.

The couple continued to go about their daily farming chores. Their garden yielded a plentiful supply of vegetables, and their crops grew exceedingly well. One day, while out in the fields, the husband and wife overheard two crows. One said, "Remember the poor corn crop in the next village?"

"Oh, how well we all remember," the other said. "We went hungry until we found this village."

"This morning a fire broke out in the dry corn fields and burned the few productive plants that were left. See the smoke to the north."

The husband and wife decided to set out to look for this mountain village to help the people. Led by smoke climbing above the tree tops, they found the smoldering fields. The villagers crowded around them and asked, "Where did you come from?"

"We live in a village which is a day's journey to the south of here," the husband said.

A woman stepped from the crowd. "That is about where we used to live. But there are two demon creatures living in our old village, a worm and a snail."

"No more," the husband said. "I used to be a worm, and my wife used to be a snail. But you see, we are like everyone else now."

"Then you are my son!" the woman said with a gasp. "Let me look at you. I cannot believe it; you are such a handsome young man. Sister! Sister!"

While the couple had a joyful reunion with their mothers, word spread quickly through the village that the former worm and snail had come to rescue them. Indeed, the husband and wife invited their mothers and all the other people to return to their former village to enjoy its prosperity. Everyone accepted.

So it was that the whole village moved back, and they all enjoyed a greater prosperity than they had ever known.

"The Worm and the Snail" is a tale from the Muong people, who live in the lower mountain regions overlooking the Red River valley. They are known as one of the ethnic minorities but are one of the largest of the highland tribes. Although their language, appearance, and customs differ from those of the Vietnamese who cling to the fertile lowlands, the Muong's language, of all the highland languages, is closest to the Vietnamese language.

Folktales often include young women who become pregnant by magical means. In Vietnam, unmarried, pregnant girls brought unbearable shame to their families, creating social pressures. Girls might no longer be recognized by their families, or they might be forced to leave their native villages for distant places where their identities would be unknown. This story is unusual in that the girls stayed at home until after they gave birth. It was then that everyone moved away, thinking the land had become contaminated by the presence of evil.

Toc Ke Stories

EYES OF A MARRIAGE

A long time ago Toc Ke, a young and very ugly, very poor man came to a small village to farm. The villagers did not want such an ugly and poor man among them, so Toc Ke received a cold welcome. He settled in a small shack on the far side of the village where people seldom had reason to go. Few knew him and none knew of his magical powers.

One day three sisters, each very beautiful, came to harvest vegetables in a nearby field. An unexpected rainstorm swept over them while they were working. They ran to the nearest shelter, Toc Ke's shack.

"Stay here out of the rain," Toc Ke said, "but I warn you I have nothing to serve, not even tea."

The sisters looked around them and saw very little food or furniture in the two-room shack. Then their eyes rested on Toc Ke's face, and the older sisters were shocked at seeing such an ugly face; they decided to walk home in the storm. The youngest sister, Ut by name, did not mind the young man's face or his bare shack and stayed until the rain passed. While she waited, she and Toc Ke talked of the coming festivals and of the village elders. Ut found that she enjoyed Toc Ke's company. By the time she left, Ut no longer saw his ugliness.

A few days later, Ut was again working in the fields when she saw a huge water buffalo bearing down upon her. In fright, she dropped everything and ran for the safety of Toc Ke's shack.

"Come and crouch behind these flowers," Toc Ke said. He immediately placed a basket of sesame seeds in his doorway. The big, hulking beast tracked Ut's footsteps to the shack and stopped at the doorway.

"Where is she?" he demanded in his deep growly voice.

"Who do you mean?" Toc Ke replied. "If you wish, you may go and look in my shack. There is no one there. But if you spill the seeds in my house, you must pick up every single one."

The beast looked first at the basket of seeds in the doorway, then beyond the door into the small shack. He stood there for a full minute before he turned and walked away. Ut was safe. As she thanked him, Toc Ke flushed and said, "I would give my life to save yours."

Realizing how much he loved her, she told her parents all about Toc Ke. They were so grateful to him for having saved Ut's life that they decided she should marry him. Ut agreed to the marriage. But, because Ut was beautiful and he was ugly, and her family was wealthy and his was not, Toc Ke, in spite of his love for her, did not feel completely secure in his marriage. Even after they had a baby son, this feeling stayed with him. He decided to test Ut's love as soon as a chance arose.

One afternoon Ut's family invited the young couple to attend a special ceremony in the village.

"I do not feel well," Toc Ke said. "Why don't you go with your family?" So Ut and their son attended with her family.

After she had left for the village, Toc Ke used his magical powers and turned himself into a handsome young man. He went to the village, looked for Ut, and flirted with her. She did not reject him. She gave him two rice cakes from the ceremony. He put the cakes away after he reached home. When Ut came home without any token of the day for him, Toc Ke was angry and jealous but said nothing.

A few moons later, Ut's parents invited them to another celebration. Toc Ke excused himself a second time and asked Ut to go with their son. Again, he turned himself into a young man, but this time, one more handsome than any the villagers had ever seen. At the festivities, he spent most of his time with Ut.

"You are so beautiful," he told her. "Why did you marry such a poor and ugly man?"

She answered with a deep sigh.

"I want to marry you," he said. "What can I do?"

"I cannot help you," she said. "When we married, my parents gave a 'bride prize' to my husband's family, and if I left my husband, we would have to pay it back. We cannot afford to do so."

"But if I had money and paid all those obligations for you, would you marry me?"

Ut looked down and said nothing. Toc Ke took her silence as consent. Sick at heart because he loved her so much, Toc Ke went home. When Ut came home, she saw how sad and ill he looked. Concerned, she suggested that they go and visit his family, who lived far away.

"How can you say that!" Toc Ke said, becoming very angry. "You do not even care for me." He changed into the first handsome young man and brought out the two rice cakes. He threw them at her. "Anybody can be handsome, but not every man will love you and take care of you." Overcome with shame, Ut began to cry.

The next day, Toc Ke woke early, packed everything he owned, and left. Ut carried their son and went to look for him. She followed the trail leading through the forest away from the village until she caught sight of him walking far ahead at a fast pace.

"Toc Ke!" she called. "Please wait for us!" But he continued walking, as if he heard nothing. When their son cried from hunger, Ut called out again. "Toc Ke! Wait for us. The baby is hungry." As angry as he was, Toc Ke loved his son, so he threw back some food.

They traveled for many days with a distance between them until they came to a river. Toc Ke used his magical powers to go across, but Ut was stranded. She cried and pleaded with the spirits of the river.

"Please help me," she said. "I have been wrong. I caused all these problems, and I am sorry. I must cross the river. Please help me."

At last a big turtle took pity on her and carried Ut and her son across the river.

Toc Ke returned to his family home, and after seven days and seven nights Ut and their son arrived, starved. Their clothes wore the dust of days.

After much discussion with his mother and deep thought, Toc Ke decided to forgive Ut.

"A husband and wife are like two eyes," he said. "If one can't see, the other is affected because both eyes look in the same direction. Like two ears, there is no such thing as the same noise sounding different to the other ear. Since you have been my wife," he went on, "we have been in the same kitchen and eaten from the same pan of rice, but your eyes have been looking elsewhere and your heart has wanted to please someone else."

Toc Ke paused, then said more slowly, "Yet you have brought our son and followed me over this long journey. I think you realize how you have behaved. If you promise to be a good and faithful wife, we shall try again to be a complete family."

Her cheeks wet with tears, Ut said, "I know I have been wrong. I shall be a good wife from now on."

Since then, for the first time in their married life, Toc Ke and Ut became a truly happy couple.

"Eyes of a Marriage" introduces the theme of testing a spouse's faithfulness. The husband's ability to transform himself into a very handsome young man makes this test an interesting one.

The "bride prize" is equivalent to the bride's dowry in other cultures.

This story originates with the Van Kieu people, a relatively small ethnic minority of the North Vietnamese highlands. As a result of the unsettled political situation, some of the Van Kieu, along with other highland groups, fled to South Vietnam during the 1960s.

HOW THE GECKO CAME TO BE

Toc Ke's son grew to be a strong and handsome young man who excelled in hunting and fishing. One day he told his parents that he wanted to hunt for elephant.

"No, no. You are too young," they said. "Let older, more experienced hunters go."

"Please, I shall be very careful," he answered. "You know I am a good hunter."

He begged so much that his parents reluctantly agreed to let him go.

In a few days he killed a couple of elephants and a few tigers. As he walked home through the forest, he met an old man who blocked his path.

"Where have you been?" the old man asked.

"I have been in the forest to kill animals that bother the villagers," the young man said.

Suddenly, in a puff of air, the old man disappeared and an elephant stood in his place, pawing the ground, ready to charge. The young man, far from being frightened, fought the elephant and had almost killed it when it vanished in another puff of air. In its place stood the old man again.

"I was testing you," he said. "You are brave and courageous. Because you have made the forest safer for the villagers, I give you a wish. Come, touch this stone that I have in my hand and wish for anything you desire."

The young man could think of nothing other than a better house for his parents. Before the thought left him, he found himself sitting in the doorway of a huge house in his village.

His grandfather, when he learned of how this wish

had come about, decided that he was old now and deserved to have a wish granted. He had always wanted a few pieces of gold to make the end of his life comfortable. So he went to the forest to look for the old man, who appeared on the path before him.

"Where have you been?" the old man asked, as he always did of strangers.

"I am old and have never had anything I wanted. Now I want you to grant me a wish," Grandfather said.

"If you want a wish fulfilled," the old man said, "you must work for it."

Unhappy at the thought that he would get no wish, Grandfather hung his head. As he did so, he saw a small object in the old man's hand, just as his grandson had described. Grandfather's hand shot out in his eagerness to touch it, but before he could the old man was gone.

Grandfather looked all around but could not find the old man. He circled the trees and rocks. He wandered here and there, searching till the light in the forest began to fade. The old man remained elusive, so Grandfather decided to go home.

He started back the way he had come, but the way was strange. He tried another trail, and again he felt no closer to home. Night was falling fast now, and he could hardly see beyond the trees. He began to call his son.

"Toc Ke! Come and help me. Toc Ke!"

Grandfather looked for the trail that led to the village, and he could not find it. Every sound in the forest startled him. He jumped behind the nearest rock at the snap of a twig. Small animals wandering across his path made Grandfather cringe in caves.

Out of hiding, he continued to call, "Toc Ke! Toc Ke!"

Throughout the day and night, Grandfather slept only in snatches. Awake, he continued to call Toc Ke and to look for the trail that would take him home.

Finally, hiding between some rocks and trees, Grandfather died. He became a gecko, afraid of everything, scurrying to hide at the slightest sound or movement, and forever calling, "Toc Ke! Toc Ke! Toc Ke!"

"How the Gecko Came to Be" illustrates the belief that one must work hard to merit what one desires. It also speaks clearly about greed that goes unrewarded while thoughtfulness is found deserving. Belief in reincarnation appears in the story when Grandfather comes back as a gecko.

Toc Ke means *gecko* and, when pronounced properly, sounds like the call of a gecko.

This tale, like "Eyes of a Marriage," comes from the Van Kieu highlanders of North Vietnam.

SPIRIT WORLD

Truong Ba and
the Butcher's Skin

Truong Ba was a master checkers player. He was so good that men from all over the country came to match their skills with his—so good, in fact, that even the best players from China came to challenge him. One day he became ill and died.

His spirit went down to Am Duong. He appeared before the King of the Dead, who checked in his book and found it was not yet time for Truong Ba to leave his earthly life.

"His death is a mistake," said the king. "Take him back to earth."

But, because he had died forty days before, his body was in no condition to take him back. Nor could he go back to Am Duong, because the demons refused to return with him. He had to look for another body.

It happened that a butcher from his village had died that morning. His wife and children were mourning him. Truong Ba spied the group and decided to slip into the butcher's body. Tears turned into surprise and laughter when the butcher stood up and said, "I must go home." He stepped out of the coffin and into the street.

"No, no. Where are you going?" the butcher's

wife said. "This is your home." She pleaded with him and followed him all the way to Truong Ba's house. He went through the front door and appeared to be perfectly at home.

He went straight to the room where he had played his checkers games. When he saw that the board had been dismantled and stored, he grumbled to himself, but he knew where everything was kept. He reassembled his board and set up the pieces to continue the play of over forty days ago.

"Husband!" the butcher's wife said, tugging at his robe. "This is not where you live. Come home with me."

"Oh, no," Truong Ba's wife said, watching him practice his game of checkers. "This is *not* your husband. He is Truong Ba, *my* husband, the master checkers player of the whole country."

The butcher's wife continued to urge him to return with her. Truong Ba's wife insisted he stay. The two women finally took their argument to a judge.

"How can you tell this is your husband?" the judge asked Truong Ba's wife.

"He is the best checkers player in the country," she replied. "Test him and you'll see."

So the judge had the best players challenge this man who looked like the butcher, and every one of them lost to him.

Then the judge asked the butcher's wife, "Why do you say this man is your husband?"

"Because he looks like my husband and he can butcher a pig very well."

A pig was brought to him. The man who played checkers like Truong Ba walked around and around the pig, not knowing where to hold it. Finally, he gained a hold on the pig, but he did not know where to cut first.

The judge's verdict was: "The spirit is Truong Ba's spirit. But the skin is that of the butcher. Truong Ba may live with his wife, but he must remember he has the butcher's body now. So he should treat the butcher's wife and children as the butcher did when he was alive."

If you had been the judge, what would you have done?

"Truong Ba and the Butcher's Skin" is a story based on a Vietnamese belief that every person has an allotted number of days on this earth.

To the Vietnamese, the spirit world was as real as the day-to-day world. Over centuries of superstition, people believed that an individual might carry the spirit of a deceased person. In the western world, some might say that the person was possessed.

A characteristic of the Vietnamese wit is displayed in this story: the difficulty of being practical in an impractical situation.

The General

There was a time long ago when the country suffered through many wars, followed by a plague that resulted in more deaths. During these unfortunate days, Di Thanh, a wise and noble man, rode his horse by fallow fields in the countryside and came upon a gathering of unhappy spirits. The starving spirits, in their search for food, roamed among the living, spreading disease and troubles.

"Why do you plan more evil?" he asked these spirits.

"We want more troops for an army," they answered.

"If you have more troops," he said, "you will need more food to feed them. And if you spread disease and illness among the living, there will be fewer living people to make food offerings to you."

The spirits began to mumble among themselves. They had not thought of this.

"I am ashamed of your behavior," Di Thanh said. "You will be punished, you know. You cannot escape."

"But we died young," they said. "Our destinies had not come to term yet. This is why we wander around as we do, looking for food."

Di Thanh felt sorry for them and invited them to a

banquet where he fed all of the starving spirits. As the spirits became acquainted with him, they recognized their own lack of leadership. They asked him to be their leader.

"If I become your leader," he said, "I must demand that you observe six taboos. The first is, you cannot disobey my orders. Second, you must not behave in a lustful manner. Third, you must not make an attempt on people's lives. Fourth, you must help people and not steal from them. Fifth, you cannot gather together at night. Sixth, you must not appear in human form during the day."

"We agree; we agree!" they all shouted.

Only one thing stood in the way: Di Thanh did not belong to the World of the Dead.

The spirits petitioned the king of the World of the Dead for Di Thanh's leadership. The king then offered Di Thanh the position of general of the army in charge of the execution of *Da Xoa*, or the criminal laws. Di Thanh accepted this position and consented to die.

Meanwhile, Le Ngo, a close friend of Di Thanh, had stopped at an inn in his search for work. One night he heard a commotion outside. He looked out his window and saw the arrival of a man clothed and hooded in black, riding a silver horse. Sitting tall in the saddle, the figure gave a command to the regiment of mounted men who followed him. Although Le Ngo recognized no one, the voice he heard was that of his dear friend Di Thanh. He hurried downstairs to see for himself.

"Di Thanh, is that you?" Le Ngo asked.

"Le Ngo!" Di Thanh said. "What are you doing here?"

"I am looking for work," Le Ngo said. "This war has taken my wealth from me. And you? Are you fighting in the army?"

"I belong to the World of the Dead now," Di Thanh answered. "I am general of the army and my responsibility is to see that the spirits follow *Da Xoa*, the criminal laws."

"So that is why you are dressed in black. I recognized only your voice."

"I wish I could help you out of poverty, but I cannot. Right now, your wife and children are in grave danger. Go home. Make many offerings to the spirits. The offerings will save your family."

Le Ngo hurried home to find his family dying of the plague. Remembering Di Thanh's advice, Le Ngo made many offerings of food. When the spirits satisfied their hunger, they relieved the family of the plague.

In thanksgiving, Le Ngo built an altar in his home for Di Thanh and made regular offerings to his friend's spirit. He knew that, because of Di Thanh, the souls of people who had committed crimes in this world were punished when they entered the World of the Dead. Their spirits could no longer re-enter this world to trouble the living.

Le Ngo never saw Di Thanh again, but through others who had seen him, he knew that Di Thanh, in a black uniform on his silver horse, enforced *Da Xoa* strictly throughout the country.

"I belong to the World of the Dead now," Di Thanh answered.

"The General" focuses upon the concept of *Da Xoa*, a set of laws in Am Duong, the World of the Dead. People feel it is unfair for those who commit crimes in this world to be free of punishment. But when the criminals' souls enter the World of the Dead they *are* punished under the laws of *Da Xoa*. These laws also rule the behavior of spirits so they cannot return to this world to trouble the living.

Offerings of food to the spirits of the deceased are traditional practices in many Asian countries. In this tale food was placed on an altar in the sitting room, probably with an incense-burning urn near it. People believed that spirits returned to enjoy the aromas of their favorite foods. This custom usually commemorated the death anniversaries of relatives, particularly parents and grandparents.

The Tea Server
from Heaven

A judge by the name of Duong Duc Cong died when he reached fifty years of age but returned to life a short time later.

"When I arrived at the Black City with the Iron Gate," he said, "I was directed to the red door of a palace. Two gentlemen in purple robes sat within. They looked at their register and told me the gods had decided to grant me two more eras of life, one era being twelve years, to continue to do good deeds."

"The night you died," his wife answered, "I had a very strange dream. A star fell from the heavens and entered me. I have never had such a dream in my life."

In time, she found that she was pregnant and gave birth to a son, Thien Tich.

Thien Tich grew up to be a learned, handsome young man who had a passion for tea. When he was twenty-four years old, his father died. Duong Duc Cong's death brought poverty to his family, which caused people to look down on them.

Thien Tich often asked, "Mother, why did Father leave us so poor? It is not fair. He helped many, many people, but he could not help his own family."

"He was honest," his mother replied, "perhaps too honest to accumulate wealth."

Thien Tich could not help feeling bitter.

He decided to look for a girl from a rich family to contract for a marriage in the future. It was common practice in those days for a young and learned but poor gentleman to do so. He moved to another village where, he believed, people would not treat his poverty with contempt. He took room and board in the home of a wealthy man.

One afternoon, as Thien Tich dozed over his books, an old mandarin appeared before him.

"Son of Duong Duc Cong," he said, "your father once saved me from trouble, and I am forever grateful to him. Now I ask you to marry my daughter Han Anh." Before Thien Tich could reply, the old mandarin disappeared, leaving a puzzled young man who was not sure if he had dreamed the whole episode.

It was not long after this that his neighbors noticed Thien Tich's handsome appearance and intellectual abilities. They arranged for his marriage to their daughter.

Although Thien Tich was very happy with his young wife, he often thought of the old mandarin. One day he told his wife about the mandarin. Her eyes grew round with surprise, then filled with tears. "I am Han Anh, the old mandarin's daughter."

"This cannot be!" Thien Tich exclaimed. "Your name is not Han Anh."

"My father had been a province chief," she said. "Because someone accused him falsely, our whole family was thrown into prison. Everyone else died there. I am alive today only because of your father.

He arranged for me to leave prison and be adopted by a wealthy family. My adopted family gave me a new name."

This bond forged in the past added to the young couple's happiness.

Thien Tich completed his studies successfully and was appointed to the position of prime minister. He was loyal to the king, but bitterness about the treatment he had received when he was poor made him seek revenge whenever the chance arose.

In his new position, Thien Tich received hundreds of religious hermits, men who left home for mountain retreats to improve themselves through prayer, meditation, and study. These men were usually well dressed in their religious robes.

One day a religious man wearing rags insisted on seeing him. Thien Tich ordered him away. Turning to leave, the religious hermit complained, "What a disloyal friend. You will regret this when misfortune comes your way."

"Wait," Thien Tich said. "Why do you say we are friends? I do not know you."

"We were friends at one time," the hermit said. "Before you came here, you were a tea server to the god in heaven and I served wine to the stars in the Palace of Stars. That is when we were friends."

"Do you mean that I was a tea server in my previous life?" Thien Tich asked.

"Yes," the hermit said. "When our god asked all his servants if someone would go to earth to be a prime minister to the king, you volunteered."

"So that is why I have such a love for tea," Thien Tich said.

"As for myself," the hermit said, "I was exiled to earth for thirty-six years because of my drunkenness. I am now at the end of my exile."

"What is the misfortune you predict?" Thien Tich asked. "And what did I do to deserve it?"

"You have held this high position too long, and you have been unusually harsh on some people," the hermit said. "You have created discontent and hatred. Although these people are now dead, their spirits are still seeking revenge."

"I see good people go unrewarded and bad people enjoy happiness and wealth," Thien Tich said. "It is not fair, so I try to reward virtue in my position."

"The gods will punish the bad people. Although punishments are slow to come," the hermit said, "they are inevitable. What we see now are the results of people's actions in their previous lives."

"What shall I do about the misfortune you say will come to me?"

"Call my name when it happens. Stay away from riches and earthly ties and concentrate on doing good deeds."

Before the hermit left, Thien Tich offered him some gold. He refused it, saying, "Your living a good and virtuous life will be the greatest gift from you."

Five years later misfortune struck. Because of a bad mistake in judgment, Thien Tich was dismissed from the king's court to fill a position in a far away province.

On his way to the new post, a storm arose. The waves rose higher and higher and the ship tossed in the turbulent waters. Lashed by howling winds, Thien Tich found himself surrounded by a crowd of demons shrieking for revenge.

Remembering the hermit, Thien Tich called out his name. Instantly, fairies riding on a carriage of clouds came to rescue him, the seas calmed, and the ship reached shore safely.

Thien Tich took this as a sign that he should devote his life to prayer and meditation. He bade farewell to his wife and children and to his life as a wealthy official of the king and disappeared into the mountains.

Leaving all riches and earthly ties, Thien Tich became a religious hermit.

"The Tea Server from Heaven" centers on a teaching of Confucius that the performance of good deeds or actions is a higher goal than the acquisition of material wealth during one's lifetime. It also demonstrates the Buddhist belief in karma, that the quality of life in a man's past affects his present life, which in turn influences future lifetimes.

Reincarnation plays a role in the story as the religious hermit reveals the positions he and Thien Tich held in their former lives. The hermit confesses to having been exiled to earth for thirty-six years for his habitual drinking. The Vietnamese, who are not heavy drinkers, consider alcoholism a social disgrace that brings dishonor.

The majority of Vietnamese are believers in Buddhism, a religion based on the teachings of Buddha. Buddha emphasized that contemplation of spiritual matters purified man's soul, enabling him to enter into nirvana, the state of eternal happiness. At the end of "The Tea Server," Thien Tich decides to practice *tu luyen* by leading a virtuous life as a religious wise man (see "The Snake Princess"). His action illustrates a Vietnamese cultural belief that one cannot avoid one's karma on earth without abandoning earthly ties and concentrating on spiritual values.

Trial in the Dragon's Palace

Once, long ago, Duong Thi, young wife of the local mandarin, traveled by boat on the river to visit her parents. She anchored her boat next to a small shrine. Similar to the dozen or more like it in the country, this temple had been built for worship of a particular kind of fish. In time, these fish spirits became very evil, causing trouble and unhappiness for people who lived nearby. No one worshiped them any more, but the shrines were left standing.

While at her parents' home, Duong Thi received a visit from two young maidens. They presented her with a beautiful golden box in which she found a panel of purple silk inscribed with a poem:

> I fell in love with your smile.
> Please wait awhile
> And I'll ready a place
> For you in the Crystal Palace.

As she read this poem, Duong Thi felt a chill run through her. She left for home right away. Her husband Trinh, the mandarin, suspected a trick. "This smells like something one of those evil fish spirits likes to do," he said. "We are doubling the security around the palace."

Six months later a terrible storm awakened Trinh in the middle of the night. He looked for Duong Thi at his side, but she was not there. He looked in and around the palace for her, but there was no sign of her. The next day her clothes were found on the river bank.

Heartbroken, Trinh resigned from his position and dug a grave for her at the foot of a mountain near the river. Because her body was never found, he held on to a thread of hope and built a watchtower positioned to give him a clear view of the river.

Every day Trinh went to this watchtower to observe the activities on and around the river. He noticed an elderly man carrying a red bag pass by every morning and retrace his steps in the evening. He followed this man one day and found that he spent the whole day palm reading at the market place. Trinh wanted to make this man's acquaintance; but, although the man was friendly, he never told Trinh his name.

Early one morning Trinh hid himself in a bush and, when the old man walked out of the water, ran out to greet him.

"Aha, you have been following me," the old man said. "Since we are friends, I do not mind telling you that I am Bach Long Hau (the Earl of White Dragon). Since this is a year of drought, I do not receive orders from the god in heaven to make rain. So, right now, I can spend all my time reading palms."

Trinh, thinking of Duong Thi, then said, "I have heard of people long, long ago who visited a palace in the sea. May I go there with you?"

"That is not hard to do," the old man said. He raised his cane and pointed it at the water. Before Trinh's eyes, the water receded to both banks, leaving a dry roadway in front of them. This path led Trinh downhill to a place where strange-looking buildings stood. These buildings had huge pockmarked tumors on the outside walls. Many branchlike arms reached out from the walls. From cave openings, sea creatures eyed them with open curiosity. Soon Trinh and the old man reached the most beautiful building that Trinh had ever seen. It was Long Hau's palace. Its jagged outer walls were a rich, deep pink. The inner walls were inlaid with mother of pearl.

Trinh was treated very kindly during his visit with Long Hau. He discussed the disappearance of his wife and expressed the hope that Long Hau could help him find her.

"Someone has done you a great wrong," Long Hau agreed, "but I cannot interfere without being punished myself, because he is assigned a rank and certain duties by the God of the Sea. And he has not bothered me, you see."

Long Hau saw Trinh's disappointment. "Let us find out exactly who the enemy is," he said. "I must find a servant who is willing to go on this mission for us."

A young servant girl volunteered. Trinh gave her a hairpin of blue pearls as a token to his wife, a sign which Duong Thi would recognize as being a message from him.

Wearing a blue dress, the girl went to the temple of the Sea Snake in the county where Trinh and Duong Thi had lived. She made inquiries and found

Many branchlike arms reached out from the walls.

that, yes, there was a woman by the name of Duong living in the Sea Snake's Crystal Palace. She was the most favored in the Sea Snake's household.

To go and see her was a difficult thing to do as the palace was well guarded. The servant girl observed that a garden of beautiful flowers surrounding the palace walls was enclosed by a high fence.

She decided on a plan. She pretended to try to reach over the fence and pick a flower growing just inside.

"Here!" the guard shouted. "You cannot pick the flowers!"

"I am sorry," the girl said, with a tremor in her voice. "I meant no harm. I have just brought a gift for the lady of the palace. Would you be so kind as to take it to her?"

Duong Thi, upon receiving the hairpin, recognized it immediately. Hope that her husband was near overwhelmed her. To hide her own feelings, she pretended to be very angry with the girl's boldness and ordered her to be thrown into jail.

As soon as the excitement over the girl had died down, Duong Thi went to see her. In tears, she asked her how she had come to possess the hairpin. She learned that Trinh was still looking for her and still hoping that she would come back. Then Duong Thi understood that if she could not or did not want to return, by the token of the hairpin, he released her of all obligations to him.

Duong Thi wrote a letter to Trinh, describing her suffering since she had been taken from his side and asking him to help her escape from her captor. She entrusted this letter to the girl and released her from jail.

Soon after, the whole affair came before the God of the Sea. The Sea Snake Spirit appeared at the trial in the form of a muscular, bearded young man with a dark, glossy skin, wearing a red headpiece. He pleaded not guilty.

As the trial progressed, the God of the Sea became angrier and angrier as he discovered that the Sea Snake Spirit had used his position and powers to take other men's wives to keep for his own. He sentenced the Sea Snake and his family to death.

"Your highness," the officer in charge of court records said, "remember that, in the past, the Sea Snake has rendered us many favors and services. I recommend a lighter sentence for him."

"Very well," the God of the Sea said. "His life is spared, but he must remain in a dark cell forever."

Duong Thi and Trinh, overjoyed to be together again, went home, while the Sea Snake Spirit left his home and fled to the north. To this day, his descendants continue to live only in dark caves.

"Trial in the Dragon's Palace" relates the story of the destructive characteristics of the Sea Snake, believed to be half snake and half man. In other tales of the Sea Snake his spirit is usually depicted as it is here, a muscular, bearded young man with a dark, glossy skin, wearing a red headpiece.

The Vietnamese hated and feared sea snakes as much as those on land (see "The Snake Princess"). There is a story about a man, Thu Phi, who was on a ship when he saw two snakes swimming alongside it. He jumped into the water, killed both snakes, and saved all on board. The king heard the story and moved Thu Phi to a position of rank at his court, thus rewarding an act of bravery that eliminated a threat to man.

The hairpin mentioned in "Trial in the Dragon's Palace" was a token of trust and confidence, as it was in the story "The

Jealous Husband." When Trinh gave his wife's hairpin to the servant girl, it was a sign that his wife could trust the girl with a message.

Based on the Vietnamese beliefs that white is a beneficial color and that dragons spit water, the Earl of White Dragon as rain-maker was aptly named.

A Strange
Encounter

Once there was a student named Ha Nhan Gia who lived in the capital city to study. Every day on his way to school, he passed an old house with crumbling garden walls. Behind these walls, among colorful, exotic plants and flowers, he always saw two young women giggling and whispering to each other. They smiled and tossed flowers to him as he walked past. The women were so beautiful that Ha often dreamed about them.

One day, after they had playfully thrown fruits and flowers to him, Ha felt brave enough to stop and talk to the two women.

"These fruits and flowers are rare. Do they grow in your garden?"

"Oh, yes." And the two giggled as they half concealed their faces behind flowers they held in their hands. "I am Lieu Thi," one said. "I am Dao Thi," the other said.

"Do you live here?" Ha asked them.

"Our master has passed away, but we continue to live here by ourselves," they said.

"If you are free this afternoon, please come and have tea with me," Ha said. "I shall come for you on my way home from school."

That evening he discovered that both women were poets. The three enjoyed writing poetry together. Ha asked them to return the next evening. The two women came, not just the next evening, but every evening after that.

Life was so pleasant that Ha often forgot to study.

When the rains ceased and the nights became warmer, the women gave a party honoring Ha. He went to their home, walking through the now familiar gate and along a fence on a path leading to a pond. Here in the open air the guests sat among rare plants surrounded by the sweet scent of flowers. As Ha looked around, he felt he was in a dream. He observed the rich silk robes worn by everyone, but failed to note their old-fashioned style.

All the guests introduced themselves to him. He sat on a mat made of woven bamboo branches and feasted on wine made of almonds and delicate pastries wrapped in fig leaves. Torches made of pine lit by pine resin cast soft shadows in the garden. He heard music but saw no musicians. The banquet went on all night, ending at daybreak.

In the midst of this amusing life, Ha received a letter from his parents asking him to come back to get married. His parents, according to custom, had arranged a marriage for him. He was very sad, but the two women urged him to go, begging that he think of them sometimes.

When he reached home, Ha agreed to marry as his parents wished. He only asked that the marriage be postponed for now. When his parents agreed, he joyfully hurried back to his friends, who were happy to know that he was faithful to them.

One night soon after his return he found them

weeping. "We have rheumatism and colds," they said. "We cannot stand bad weather. We think our lives are going to end here."

"What can I do?" the young man asked. "I will do anything to help you."

"You can do nothing," they said. "That is our destiny. Very soon now, when the next storm comes, we'll be gone."

A big storm did come the very next night. Ha was so upset that he couldn't stay by himself. He went to see his neighbor, an old man, and told him of his friendship with the two women.

"Are you dreaming?" the old man said. "There used to be a mandarin living there twenty years ago, but no one has lived there for many years now. Those two women must be bad women or bad ghosts who are out to do you mischief."

The old man went with Ha to the garden the next morning. It was deserted. Weeds grew everywhere and all but choked the plants. Ha looked around in a daze. He mentioned the names of the ladies and gentlemen who had been guests at the banquet. The old man pointed out the plants and flowers in the garden with those same names. Ha then knew that his friends had been spirits and he had been living in a dream world.

Realizing how much he had neglected his studies, he blamed himself for wasting so much time seeking pleasure. He then pawned one of his robes to pay for offerings and arranged for a ceremony in the garden. He knew that restless spirits could have peace only after special prayers and offerings were made.

That night the women appeared in a dream. "We are so grateful for what you did today," they said.

"We have had a wonderful time with you, but our destiny is light and fragile and life is easily blown away. Thank you and good-bye, good-bye."

Ha was filled with a longing to see them again. He got up to touch once more the shoes they had left as souvenirs. As he picked them up, his hands held only petals which drifted through his fingers, leaving them empty.

"A Strange Encounter," perhaps more than any other tale in this collection, has an ethereal quality that shows the influence of the Chinese upon the Vietnamese.

Poetry writing, noted in the first part of the story, was a highly regarded pastime, the mark of a learned person. The filial piety advocated by Confucius enters the story when Ha Nhan's parents arrange a marriage for him. Deeply attached to his family, the young man has no choice but to consent to the marriage.

The Story
of Le Nuong

Le Nuong and Phat Sinh were promised to each other in marriage soon after they were born. Their mothers, close friends and neighbors for years, wanted their children to marry each other.

Although it was unusual for parents to allow a boy and girl to play together, the two children spent much time with each other as they grew up. As a result, a strong love developed between the two. Before they could marry, war broke out, and Le Nuong, along with other women relatives of the defeated ruler, was taken as a servant into the enemy camp. As she was about to leave the village, she begged Phat Sinh, "Please marry someone else. It may be a long time before I can return."

"I love you, Le Nuong," Phat Sinh said. "I cannot think of marrying anyone else. I shall try to rescue you."

"And if you cannot rescue me, please do not wait for me," she said.

They knew that this was an unsettled time for their country, with different leaders warring against each other and the Chinese invading from the north.

Unfortunately, before Phat Sinh could do anything, Le Nuong was captured again, this time by the Chinese invaders.

In order to rescue Le Nuong, Phat Sinh offered his king a plan that would stop the Chinese from advancing farther south. The king used Phat Sinh's strategy successfully, but it brought Sinh no closer to Le Nuong. So he left the army to search for her on his own.

One evening, close to a deserted military post, he met an old woman who remembered a person of Le Nuong's description.

"She was with two other young women," she said. "When the troops and all the prisoners came closer to the border, the three preferred to die and be buried in their own country rather than to live in China, an enemy country."

Sinh discovered that the three women were buried in the mountain. After many days of searching for their graves, he found them in a quiet spot off the footpath. He spent the night there and prayed that Le Nuong would appear in his dreams that night.

She came to him, weeping. "I am sorry," she said. "I am heartbroken that we cannot marry, but I refuse to be a concubine in a Chinese court. I did the only thing I could to avoid that fate."

"My heart breaks when I think of your suffering," Phat Sinh said, "but you did what you must do. Shall I take you home to be buried?"

"I have been with my two friends through many hardships," she said. "We have become close to each other, and we enjoy this place. It is quiet and has a wonderful view of the valley. I wish to stay here."

They spent the rest of the night together, reliving their past happiness. The next day, Phat Sinh bought three coffins at the nearest village and reburied the remains of the three women. That night the three women visited briefly to thank him. Sadly, he left for home as soon as day dawned.

Always faithful to Le Nuong, Phat Sinh never married.

"The Story of Le Nuong" takes place during a period of turmoil from frequent wars. It was a time when Ho Qui Ly, an imposter, ruled Vietnam in place of its rightful king, Tran. When Tran Khat-chan, a loyal servant and mandarin of Tran's court and a relative of Le Nuong, attempted to capture the imposter, his plot was discovered and he was executed. To add to the confusion, China had meanwhile become involved in the internal strife of Vietnam and had invaded that country.

It was the custom in those days that, when two armies fought, the victorious leader not only acquired the enemy soldiers but also gained as servants or concubines the women relatives of the vanquished one. Thus, Le Nuong was taken by the victors.

FOOD, LOVE,
AND LAUGHTER

Rice Cakes
for the New Year

Under the reign of King Hung Vuong VI, a time when people thought the sky was round and the earth square, a king could have more than one wife, and Hung Vuong had many.

As he aged, Hung Vuong became tired of ruling the kingdom, and he puzzled over which of his twenty-two sons should take over his throne. After much thought, he called all twenty-two princes to his court.

"Go out through the land," he ordered, "and find a food so unusual that I have never tasted it before. The one who brings me the best and most unusual dish will become king. You shall have one whole season to find it."

He hoped his sons would go out and learn how their people lived. Twenty-one princes scattered throughout the kingdom. Only one, Lang Lieu, the sixteenth son of the king, stayed home.

Lang Lieu excelled in hunting, as well as in the writing of poetry. He loved challenges of all kinds, but he did not want to leave home. His nursemaid, who had taken the place of the mother he had lost when he was born, was very ill, and Lang Lieu was reluctant to leave her bedside. Every day he worried about the king's decree.

One night he dreamed he saw a thin old man whose wisp of a beard was as white as the clouds. The old man told Lang Lieu that he was a genie come to help him solve the problem the king had posed.

"In this world," he said, "there is nothing more precious than rice. Use rice to cook a dish for the king. Make the rice represent earth and sky so that the people eating it will appreciate both."

Then the old man disappeared. Lang Lieu pondered over his dream. He decided to call his court to seek their counsel. They discussed, argued, and finally decided to make a dish using rice that was newly harvested, meat that represented the richness of the land, and the yellow mung beans that grew plentifully in the country.

After much experimenting, they put the ingredients together. Raw uncooked rice was spread in a single layer, upon which a layer of mung beans was placed. On these beans a layer of pork was spread, followed by another layer of beans, which in turn was covered with a last layer of rice. All of this was wrapped and tied in green banana leaves and shaped into either a square block or a cylinder about six inches long. Then these round or square bundles were placed in a pot of water and cooked all day.

Winter passed and spring came. All twenty-two princes reassembled at court, where the king tasted every dish. When he unwrapped Lang Lieu's offering, the king found rice that had taken the green color of the banana leaf and reminded him of the green of the rice plant ripe for harvesting. He found the mung beans the royal color of yellow. The king took one bite, then another. It tasted as delightful as it looked.

"Where did you find out how to make this dish?" he asked Lang Lieu.

"I did not leave my court," Lang Lieu confessed. "While I worried about finding a dish for you, I had a dream in which a genie came to give me this idea. The round cake is sky and the square, the earth."

The king was overjoyed to hear this because, besides possessing intelligence, Lang Lieu had received guidance from heaven. Such guidance was most fortunate for a king to have, and receiving it was a rare event. Hung Vuong named the square-shaped cake *banh chung* and the round *banh day*.

"This shows me," the king said, "that the gods will help you rule wisely." So Lang Lieu was named to succeed the king. Hung Vuong also proclaimed to all his people that they make *banh chung* and *banh day* as Lang Lieu had made them.

Lang Lieu taught the people how to make *banh chung* and *banh day*, and in this way to give thanks to the earth and the sky for all their blessings.

"Rice Cakes for the New Year" tells how the Vietnamese came to greet each New Year with special rice cakes. These cakes take hours to prepare, and their ingredients are symbolic. Because many pigs were raised on the deltas, pork was chosen to show the richness of the countryside. The plentiful mung beans were selected because they were yellow, the color of royalty, while in the cooking process the green banana leaves gave color to the rice, representing the green of a good rice harvest.

The cakes are symbolic in shape as well. The round cakes depict the sky and the square ones, the earth, thus fulfilling the genie's suggestion to the sixteenth prince in his dream, and also portraying the people's belief at that time about the shapes of earth and sky.

To this day, the Vietnamese celebrate Tet, the lunar calendar New Year, as their most important holiday. It is celebrated sometime between January and March, depending on the lunar cycle, and lasts a minimum of three days, with stores and businesses closed in observance. Although Tet is not a religious holiday, it is colored by religious practices. Many people go to temples to pray for health, prosperity, longevity, and happiness in the New Year.

At home, the head of the family performs rituals before an altar to worship Buddha, various ancestors, and gods, and to pray for the New Year. Children stay up late to receive money gifts supposedly commensurate with their conduct and performance during the past year. Because whatever is said or takes place on the first day of the year is expected to repeat itself and influence people's lives throughout the year, the Vietnamese strictly avoid bad things on that day.

Two Brothers

During the reign of Hung Vuong IV, there were two brothers, Tan and Lang, who looked exactly alike. They were not twins, but even their own mother had trouble telling them apart. Tall and handsome, both had the same black wavy hair that curled when wet and the same high bridge on the nose. Their voices sounded alike. They even walked with the same gait. They did things together and went everywhere together.

When the older brother was eighteen years of age, their parents died. The brothers went to stay with the mandarin Luu, an old friend of the family who had agreed to oversee the rest of their education. Luu's beautiful daughter Xuan Phu, attracted to their handsome features and amiable characters, thought of a way to tell the older from the younger brother.

When she set the table, she placed only one pair of chopsticks before the brothers. Because it was the custom to respect one's elders and defer to them, Lang always gave the chopsticks to Tan. After Tan ate, Lang washed the chopsticks, and had his meal. Then Xuan Phu knew which was Tan and which was Lang.

Before long, Tan fell in love with Xuan Phu. Lang

also fell in love with her, but because Tan was older and wanted to marry her, Lang kept his feelings to himself.

Tan married Xuan Phu, and Lang continued to live with them. He laid aside his feelings for Xuan Phu and began to treat her like a sister. But he missed Tan's companionship and felt shut out of his life, because Tan now spent all of his time with Xuan Phu.

One day the two brothers went hunting. Lang was overjoyed to be with his brother, but he tired before Tan so he came home first. Xuan Phu, believing him to be her husband, ran to greet him, throwing her arms around him and showing him her love and affection.

Lang was too embarrassed to tell Xuan Phu of her mistake. He was sure that he had shown his love for her by something he had said or done, and he felt guilty. He knew he could no longer stay with Tan and Xuan Phu.

He left the house before Tan got home and began to walk. He kept walking through day and night, into the forest and over the mountain, until he reached a wide river. He sorely missed his brother. But, physically exhausted and mentally despairing, he collapsed and fell into a deep sleep. He never awakened. His body turned into a white boulder on the bank of the river.

When Tan came home from the hunting trip, his wife ran out to greet him.

"Oh, Husband!" she said. "I have made a terrible mistake." She told him what she had done and how Lang had left home.

"Poor Lang," Tan said. "I have neglected him lately. I must find him and bring him back."

Tan walked and he walked, asking everyone he met, "Have you seen my brother? He looks exactly like me." Lang was always just ahead of him.

Tan kept walking through day and night into the same forest where Lang had walked and over the same mountain. He reached the same river that Lang had reached. With every mile he walked, he missed Lang more and more. He realized how much he had neglected his brother and how much he missed him now.

Tan was weak from hunger and exhaustion; he had not expected to walk so far. He sat on the white rock on the side of the river and felt a great sense of hopelessness wash over him. Overcome with grief for his brother, he collapsed, and he, too, died on the same spot. In his place, an areca palm tree, sprouting leaves and nuts at its top, grew tall and straight.

For many days Xuan Phu waited for her husband and his brother. She worried, pacing back and forth in the house, unable to eat anything. Finally, she could wait no longer and set out to look for them. Through the village, into the same forest, and over the same mountain she walked. She asked everyone she met, "Have you seen my husband or his brother? They look exactly alike." People always pointed ahead; everybody had seen them go by. When she arrived at the same river, she, too, stopped.

Hungry, tired, and thoroughly discouraged, she sat on the white rock and leaned on the tall palm tree growing beside it. Exhausted, she slowly collapsed against the palm tree and died on that spot.

Her body became a betel vine that curled and wove itself around the palm tree.

Her body became a betel vine that curled and wove itself around the palm tree.

People in the nearby town soon noticed that, in monsoon, typhoon, flood, or drought, the areca palm and the betel plant always survived. While everything else died, the areca and betel remained green. This surprising fact, together with the story of the two brothers and Xuan Phu, spread from town to town until it reached the ears of the king.

"What love and devotion!" the king said. "There is an old saying: the blood of related persons, mixed in a bowl, will clot or come together in a mass. Let us use this test with the rock, the tree, and the plant. Then we will see if this story is really true and the young people are related."

So the betel leaf, the areca nut, and scrapings from the white rock were pounded together. The blend produced a juice the color of blood. The king was convinced.

"The areca nut, the betel leaf, and limestone powder," the king proclaimed, "stand for fidelity between brothers even after marriage and celebrate the devotion of husband and wife."

He ordered the villagers and all his subjects to use these three—the betel leaf, the areca nut, and powdered limestone—as an offering before marriage. When the people tasted it, they liked it so well that they immediately followed the king's order. Ever since, every bridegroom's family includes a plate of the sliced nut, betel leaves as a wrapper, and powdered limestone mixed to a paste with other gifts for the bride-to-be.

"Two Brothers" is an example of the cultural practice, based on a teaching of Confucius, of respecting one's elders—in this instance, an older brother. The tale also emphasizes the importance of betel nuts and the seeds of the areca palm in Vietnamese society. The nuts are gathered before they are quite ripe, then husked, boiled, cut into slices, and dried in the sun. For chewing, a small piece is wrapped in a leaf of the betel pepper, with a pellet of lime to cause salivation and to release the stimulating alkaloids. Chewing produces a copious flow of brick-red saliva that is not swallowed, the effect being that of a mild stimulant.

Even today, when a young man asks for a girl's hand in marriage, if he observes traditional customs, a plate of the sliced nut wrapped in betel leaves and powdered limestone mixed to a paste accompanies other gifts to the family of the bride-to-be. It appears again at weddings, on birthdays, at New Year's, and on an anniversary of the dead, because the betel leaf, areca nut, and limestone together symbolize family fidelity.

The Lady
of Stone

A long time ago, by the South China Sea, there was a family of fishermen with an only daughter by the name of Ba. *Ba* was a name often given to the second-born, yet she was raised as an only child. Many times she asked her parents, "Do I have an older brother or sister?" They ignored her question and said nothing.

One day, when she asked the same question again, they replied, "When you were three years old, your brother Hai was five. You fought over a piece of sugarcane. Hai hit you so hard with the sugarcane that you fainted and started to bleed. Hai was frightened and ran away from home. We have never seen him since."

Ba wished that her brother Hai was with them now. As she grew older, she knew her father also wished that Hai were there to help him. Ba felt responsible for Hai's absence.

When Ba reached the age of thirteen, she offered to go out in the boat with her parents.

"No, we cannot allow it," they said. "The work is hard, and the sea is treacherous. You cannot go with us."

115

That same year her parents were caught in a
typhoon at sea. Ba went down to the seashore every
day and waited for them to come home. Every day
she watched other fishermen come back to their
families. Her parents never returned.

Ba finally knew that she would never see them
again. She left her village to go to Phu Yen where her
uncle lived. But when she got there, she found that
her uncle had moved, and no one could tell her
where he had gone.

Again, Ba felt all alone. This time, instead of
looking for her uncle, Ba looked for work. She
became a helper in a fishmarket. Day after day she
worked hard.

When she reached eighteen, she met and fell in
love with a young fisherman. They were married. Ba
began to go fishing with her husband, just as her
mother had accompanied her father. They owned
their fishing boat and, working together, stayed out
on the ocean for days at a time. They did not return
to shore until the boat was loaded with fishes, clam,
lobster, shrimp, and other seafood. Soon they could
afford a bigger and better house to replace their old
thatched hut. They bought a larger, more sturdy
boat, and Ba was able to have a housekeeper.

Since Ba was now expecting their first child,
instead of going out in the boat she remained ashore
and took charge of selling their catch. Her husband,
overjoyed at having a child, worked harder than
ever. These were happy years for both of them. The
loneliness of the past seemed to Ba like a nightmare,
never to be repeated, for she was so much in love
with her husband.

When the typhoon season came, the wind changed

direction and whipped eastward. The waves were often over ten feet high. This was the season when all fishermen stayed home. Ba's husband, restless without work to do, watched her as she washed her hair.

"Here, let me help you," he said.

He helped to rinse her hair, then ran the comb through it.

"What is this scar?" he asked. The scar was at the base of her skull, well covered by hair.

"Oh, that," Ba said. "I almost forgot I had that scar." Taking the comb from his hands, she continued to comb her hair while she told her story.

"I do not remember my brother, but my parents told me that he and I fought over a piece of sugarcane. He grabbed it and hit me on the head with it and left me bleeding and in a faint. He ran away, and we never saw him again." Her husband listened as if transfixed. Ba suddenly realized that her husband had a strange look on his face.

"Is anything the matter?" she asked. "Did I say something to upset you?"

"No," he said. He did not say more.

"I know I have upset you dreadfully. Please tell me what is wrong," she said, but he said nothing.

That night his thoughts were in a turmoil. How could it be mere coincidence, he thought—the fight over a piece of sugarcane, the wound in the head, and the brother who ran away—all things that he remembered so well from the time he was five years old and ran away? He could not stand the thought that kept coming to him. Was it possible? he asked himself. The incidents were identical, but she would be filled with guilt and remorse if he told her.

So, without a word, he left the house and took the boat out onto an ocean that mirrored his rage.

He gazed back at the shore and silently bade farewell to his wealth, his dream, and the two people he loved most in the world, while the eastbound wind blew him farther and farther away from shore.

The next morning Ba looked for her husband but could not find him. When she saw the boat missing, she knew he had gone out to sea. As she had done once before, she went to the seashore every day and watched all the boats come in. The beach was not big enough to contain her longing for her husband, so Ba climbed to the top of Mount Deo Ca. With her newborn son in her arms, she waited, and her eyes searched the waters. She stood there in the cold and the rain, week after week, month after month. Soon the cold mountain winds turned them both to stone, and people began to call her the Lady of Stone.

Fishermen often called out to her when they had a boat heavy with a rich catch and had difficulty bringing the boat to shore. At these times, they lifted their voices to her, singing:

> Dear Lady, blow the East Wind
> Which pushes my boat,
> That will offer your husband
> A ride back home.

She is still there with her son, high on a mountain top between Da Nang and Cam Ranh Bay, looking out to sea, waiting for her husband.

"The Lady of Stone" is a tale from Vietnam's early history when many people were farming, fishing, and hunting folk. Those who lived along the sea coast became maritime people who lived by fishing, at the mercy of typhoons and their tolls of lost lives.

People still point to the stone formation on the mountain between Da Nang and Cam Ranh Bay and say that the Lady of Stone is waiting for her husband.

The Magic Crossbow

The story of Mi Chau and Trong Thuy and the magic crossbow begins over two thousand years ago with a war between the kingdoms of Van Lang and Thuc. The ruler of Thuc wanted to marry a princess from the ruling family of Van Lang, and he had been rejected. Insulted, he vowed to take revenge.

The prolonged war that followed saw the ruling family of Van Lang remain victorious for several generations until the reign of the eighteenth king, who became lax and lazy. The king of Thuc captured Van Lang. He merged the two kingdoms into one and named the new country Au Lac and himself An Duong Vuong.

An Duong Vuong had one daughter, Mi Chau, whom he treasured. He also possessed a magic crossbow that killed thousands with a single arrow. This, too, he treasured.

The crossbow owed its peculiar power to a toenail belonging to Kim Quy, guardian of the sea animals, a being with magical powers. He had come to help An Duong Vuong to build a capital city for the new nation of Au Lac. When he gave his toenail to An Duong Vuong, Kim Quy, who took the form of a golden turtle, instructed him to use the toenail in the trigger of a crossbow. With the help of a special craftsman, An Duong Vuong fashioned a bow using the toenail in its design. He also made arrows to match the bow's strength.

Because of this bow, no one could defeat him. Whenever King Trieu Da, his enemy to the north, attacked, An Duong Vuong always won. Trieu Da eventually decided that he could win only by wit and not by force. He bided his time.

When Trieu Da's son Trong Thuy was old enough, he sent him to Au Lac to draw up terms for peace and to discover An Duong Vuong's weakness. Of all his sons, Trong Thuy was the most personable. Trieu Da was confident that Trong Thuy could accomplish this task.

"You must never forget that your primary mission is to find An Duong Vuong's weakness," Trieu Da said.

"That mission will be foremost in whatever I do," Trong Thuy replied. "I promise never to forget."

The young prince made many trips between Au Lac and his own country. In the course of these missions, he met and fell in love with An Duong Vuong's only daughter, Mi Chau. She returned his love. Both kings agreed to the match, An Duong Vuong because he wanted to add to his lands and Trieu Da to find his enemy's weakness.

Mi Chau and Trong Thuy married and lived in An Duong Vuong's palace. An extremely devoted couple, they were very happy in their married life. But the young prince never forgot his promise to his father.

One night he said, "I am amazed at how your father's army can kill thousands of soldiers in a short time. What is the secret that the army possesses?"

"There is no secret," Mi Chau said. "His success is not due to the talent of the soldiers. Father has a magic crossbow."

"I am curious to see such a wonderful weapon. Is it possible for me to see it?"

"Of course," Mi Chau said. "Let me get it for you."

She brought the crossbow to show her husband and explained its magical power. Trong Thuy examined the bow carefully and memorized its design before returning it to his wife.

The next day he left to visit his father. He gave Trieu Da a report about the crossbow and sketched it so that his father's craftsman could make an identical one.

In a few days the duplicate was completed, and Trong Thuy concealed it in his bags.

"Exchange the crossbows soon after your return," Trieu Da said. "When you bring us the magic crossbow, we will attack Au Lac."

When Trong Thuy reached An Duong Vuong's palace, the king gave a welcoming banquet because Mi Chau was so happy to have her husband back. At the banquet, Trong Thuy kept serving wine to his wife and her father, while he himself had none. That night when everyone slept, Trong Thuy slipped into the king's chambers to exchange the crossbows.

The next morning Mi Chau sensed a restlessness in her husband.

"Is there something wrong?" she asked. "You are unusually restless."

"Forgive me, my dear," he said, "but my father

wants me to go on a mission to inspect his soldiers at the northern posts. I am sad to leave you again and do not wish to go, especially since I may be gone for close to a year."

"I do not want to lose you for even a day, but if you have work to do, you must do it. Do not worry about me," Mi Chau said.

But as the time drew nearer for his departure, she began to feel as restless as her husband. Uneasy, she said, "If anything should happen, and I must leave this palace, I shall take my embroidered silk coat of goose down and make a trail of feathers so you can find me."

At the last moment, she clung weeping to her husband, unwilling to let him go.

Trong Thuy also felt a foreboding, as he held his wife close to him in farewell.

A few days after he reached his father with the stolen crossbow, Trieu Da gave the order to attack Au Lac.

"So," An Duong Vuong said, "he is trying again." Unconcerned, he prepared himself for battle. When the enemy came close to the city walls, he climbed the ramparts and let his arrow fly from the crossbow. To his surprise and horror, his single arrow killed one, not thousands. The second arrow again killed only one. He realized he had been betrayed! The enemy began to close in.

Throwing his daughter onto his horse behind him, An Duong Vuong fled from the palace just as the enemy stormed his gates. They pounded the pathways fast through the forest. Whenever he slackened his pace, thinking he had outrun the enemy, he heard the sound of hooves close behind him. He reached the dark sea and looked for a ship but saw none. An Duong Vuong kept riding along the shore, trying to evade his pursuers, but the enemy was always right behind him.

He prayed out loud to Kim Quy to come and help him. Kim Quy, the huge turtle, appeared and said, "Your enemy is behind you on your own horse. I cannot help you." Then he sank back into the water.

An Duong Vuong looked back and saw his own daughter. Tears were streaming down her face as she left a trail of goose feathers behind them. He quickly unsheathed his sword and cut off her head, then followed Kim Quy into the ocean.

Meanwhile, Trong Thuy had entered the palace and immediately gone to look for his wife. He could not find her but found, instead, the trail of feathers she had promised. Though he rode very hard, he caught up to her just as An Duong disappeared into the water. And there on a lonely, windswept shore with the gray waves washing away Mi Chau's blood, Trong Thuy found her body. Weeping, he carried her tenderly back to the palace, where he buried her.

For days, Trong Thuy wandered through the palace. He spent hours fingering Mi Chau's clothes and jewelry, inhaling her presence, and recalling happy days spent in those rooms. He wandered through the palace gardens where he had once walked with her, teased her, and made her laugh. He remembered how, in her innocence, she had betrayed her father and country to her husband whom she deeply loved.

Like a man out of his mind, Trong Thuy drifted from room to room in the palace, day and night. He could not sleep; he could not eat. One day he wandered to the well where Mi Chau had taken her daily baths. He threw himself into the deep water, thus ending his tortured days.

"The Magic Crossbow" has both historical and legendary sources. An Duong Vuong, ruler of Au Lac, a large kingdom in existence before Vietnam became a nation, was one of the sons of the legendary union of the dragon king (Lac Long Quan) and the princess of the fairies (Au Co). At the time of his reign, An Duong determined that a walled citadel was necessary to protect the kingdom against enemy invasions.

Construction on the citadel, known as Co-loa or Co-loa Thanh, was delayed because each day's work was mysteriously removed during the night by spirits led by a thousand-year-old chicken perched on a nearby mountain. Finally, a golden turtle appeared, overcame the chicken, and remained with An Duong Vuong until the citadel was completed. Upon leaving, the turtle gave one of his toenails, or claws, to be used as a trigger on the king's crossbow, with the promise that the king would be invincible thereafter.

This tale explains the defeat of An Duong Vuong in 207 B.C. by his enemy, the Chinese general Trieu Da, then governor of a large province in southeastern China. The incident marked the opening of Vietnam's door to China and the eventual one-thousand-year subjugation to China.

Legend tells us that the daughter's blood flowed into the water, where it entered oysters and formed pearls. The Vietnamese believed that suicide was an appropriate end for the young husband, because he had been torn between duty and love. For many young Vietnamese trapped between filial piety and love, suicide at one time was a common solution.

They Ran to Me

One hot and humid summer day, a mandarin came home tired, his clothes wringing with perspiration. Beads of sweat rolled down his face and back; his robe was dripping. As soon as he stepped into his house, he called his servant boy, telling him to bring the fan.

The fan was huge. The boy had to hold it with both hands to fan his master. Very soon the mandarin felt much better. He glanced down and saw that even his robe was dry.

"What did you do?" he asked the servant boy. "I have cooled off already and even my robe has dried so quickly. There are no more beads of perspiration running down my back!"

"Sir," the servant boy said, "they ran to me."

"Sir," the servant boy said, "they ran to me."

Just One Ghost

The king of Am Duong had a son who was very ill. Nobody in the kingdom of Am Duong could cure him; no medicine could make him well. The king was worried because he did not want his son's condition to worsen, for there was also a kind of death in Am Duong.

So the king sent one of his subjects to earth to look for a good doctor. He told the messenger that to select the right doctor to bring back with him, he must look at the house where the doctor does his work.

"Bring the doctor who has no spirits, or ghosts, standing in line outside his house," he said.

The messenger went up to earth where he searched all over for a good doctor. Each doctor, he found, had long lines of ghosts standing outside his house. He could not find the good doctor his king had asked him to find.

After combing the villages and finding none, the discouraged messenger was almost ready to give up when he came upon a doctor with only one ghost in line. Delighted with the success of his mission, the messenger speedily took him to Am Duong and presented the doctor to the king.

The king was overjoyed. Now his son would get well.

"You must be a very good doctor to have just one ghost outside your house," he said. "Tell me, how long have you been in practice?"

"I am honored by your confidence in me," the good doctor answered. "I opened my practice today and have just one patient."

The Grateful
Tombstone

Long ago, when the principal weapon in warfare was the bow and arrow, there was an officer in the army who was proud of his ability as an archer. He was loud in his own praise and always talked about bows and arrows, shooting, and warfare.

Walking daily from his home to the military garrison where he worked, he always passed a cemetery. A particular tombstone in the cemetery was the target of the officer's daily practice with his bow and arrow. Every day on his way to work, he was sure to practice his skill by shooting a few arrows. Every day he took careful aim at the tombstone before letting his arrow fly. In spite of a mere distance of twenty meters, his arrow missed its mark. Try as he might, every single day, the officer could never hit the tombstone.

War came. The officer and his men went to the front lines. They fought hard, but fortune turned against them. His men ran back in full retreat, with the officer himself throwing everything down and running with them. While he was running, a giant of a man suddenly appeared and carried him to safety.

"Who are you?" the officer asked. "I do not even know you, but I owe my life to you."

"You know me," the stranger said. "I am the guardian spirit of the tombstone. All those years that you pretended to shoot at the tombstone, you always aimed too low or too high and never hit me. I came to help you because I owe my life to you."

The Musician

There once was a young man who played the *dan bau*, a one-stringed musical instrument. Whenever he played it, his neighbor, a young widow, cried.

She must be very touched by my playing, he thought.

To assure himself that her crying was related to his playing, he stopped playing when she started to cry. Her crying also stopped. If he played again, she cried again.

My playing must be very good, indeed, he thought. I must meet her.

One day he did meet her.

"Every time I play, I have noticed that you cry," he said. "If my playing brings back sad memories or if the music makes you sad, let me know and I shall stop playing."

"When I hear your music," the woman said, "it reminds me of my husband."

The young man was flattered.

"Then your husband must have been a talented player," he said.

"Oh, no," she said. "My husband's work was to beat the shell around the cotton boll to break the cover. He did not know how to play the *dan bau*, either."

There once was a young man who played the dan bau . . .

"They Ran to Me," "Just One Ghost," "Grateful Tombstone," and "The Musician" are representative of the lighthearted stories that are a great source of amusement for the Vietnamese, whose fondness for humor is a national characteristic.

The *dan bau*, because of its single string, is a difficult musical instrument to master but, in the hands of a competent musician, is very melodic.

SOURCES

"How the Tiger Got Its Stripes," "Tam and Cam," "Da Trang Crab," "Rice Cakes for the New Year," "The Magic Crossbow," "They Ran to Me," "Just One Ghost," "The Grateful Tombstone," and "The Musician" are from *Truyen Co Dan Gian Viet Nam* by Vu Ngoc Phan, published by Educational Publishing, Hanoi, 1972.

"Under the Starfruit Tree," and "Two Brothers" are from *Van-Hoc Binh-Dan* by Nguyen-Truc-Phuong, published by Nha Sach Khai-Tri, Saigon, 1970.

"The Jealous Husband," "The General," "A Strange Encounter," and "The Story of Le Nuong" are from *Tan Bien Truyen Ky Man Luc* by Nguyen Tu, published by Bo Giao-Duc, Ministry of Education, Center for Educational Materials, Hanoi, 1970.

"The Snake Princess," "Mister Thirty," and "Truong Ba and the Butcher's Skin" are from *Viet Nam Truyen Ky Tap Truyen* by Toan Anh, published by Que Huong, Toronto, Canada, 1985 (reprint of an earlier book published in Vietnam).

"Toc Ke I: Eyes of a Marriage," and "Toc Ke II: How the Gecko Came to Be" are from *Truyen Co Van Kieu* by Mai Van Tan, published by Nha Xuat Ban, Van Hoa Dan Toc, Hanoi, 1978.

"How the Dao People Came to Be" is from *Truyen Co Dao* by Doan Thanh, Le Trung Vu, Tran Nguyen, and Nguyen Ha, published by Nha Xuat Ban, Van Hoa Dan Toc, Hanoi, 1978.

"The Worm and the Snail" is from *Truyen Co Muong* by Hoang Anh Nhan, Vuong Anh, and Bui Thien, published by Nha Xuat Ban, Van Hoa Dan Toc, Hanoi, 1978.

"The Tea Server from Heaven," and "Trial in the Dragon's Palace" are from *Truyen Ky Man Luc* by Nguyen Du, published by Nha Xuat Ban, Van Hoc, Hanoi, 1971.

"War between Gods" and "The Lady of Stone" are from *Truyen Co Nuoc Nam* by Nguyen Dat Thinh. Translated for us by author.

"The Scholar Be" is from *Ong Do Be* by Khai-Hung.